BRITISH FURNITURE
1880~1915

Pauline Agius

Published by the
Antique Collectors' Club

British Library CIP Data.
Agius, Pauline.
    British Furniture, 1880-1915.
    1. Furniture – Great Britain – History
    I. Title II. Antique Collectors' Club.
    749.2'941   NK2530

    ISBN 0 902028 76 6

Printed in England by Baron Publishing
Church Street, Woodbridge, Suffolk

THE ANTIQUE COLLECTORS' CLUB

The Antique Collectors' Club, formed in 1966, pioneered the provision of information on prices for collectors. The Club's magazine *Antique Collecting* was the first to tackle the complex problems of describing to collectors the various features which can influence prices. In response to the enormous demand for this type of information the *Price Guide Series* was introduced in 1968 with **The Price Guide to Antique Furniture**, a book which broke new ground by illustrating the more common types of antique furniture, the sort that collectors could buy in shops and at auctions, rather than the rare museum pieces which had previously been used (and still to a large extent are used) to make up the limited amount of illustrations in books published by commercial publishers. Many other price guides have followed, all copiously illustrated, and greatly appreciated by collectors for the valuable information they contain, quite apart from prices.

Club membership, which is open to all collectors, costs £6.95 per annum. Members receive free of charge *Antique Collecting,* the Club's magazine (published every month except August), which contains well-illustrated articles dealing with the practical aspects of collecting not normally dealt with by magazines. Prices, features of value, investment potential, fakes and forgeries are all given prominence in the magazine.

In addition members buy and sell among themselves; the Club charges a nominal fee for introductions but takes no commission. Since the Club started many thousands of antiques have been offered for sale privately. No other publication contains anything to match the long list of items for sale privately which appears in each issue of the magazine.

The presentation of useful information and the facility to buy and sell privately would alone have assured the success of the Club, but perhaps the feature most valued by members is the ability to make contact with other collectors living nearby. Not only do members learn about the other branches of collecting but they make interesting friendships. The Club organises weekend seminars and other meetings.

As its motto implies, the Club is an amateur organisation designed to help collectors to get the most out of their hobby: it is informal and friendly and gives enormous enjoyment to all concerned.

For Collectors   —   By Collectors   —   About Collecting

The Antique Collectors' Club, 5 Church Street, Woodbridge, Suffolk.

Acknowledgements

The field of furniture history is remarkable for its open and ready sharing of information and advice. This stems from the generous approach of some of the subject's pioneers, notably Edward Joy, and is fostered by the vision and scholarship of Peter Thornton and his gifted team in the Department of Furniture and Woodwork at the Victoria and Albert Museum. I am indebted to many and especially wish to thank:

Elizabeth Aslin for her pioneer work *Nineteenth Century English Furniture*

Edward Joy for stimulating discussions, valuable information and continual thoughtful encouragement

Christopher Gilbert for perceptive criticism and generous help

Dr. Penelope Eames, Simon Jervis and John Hardy for advice on various chapters

Mrs. E.E. Joy and Mrs. P.M. Wager for helping to eliminate some jargon and jumbled thoughts

Anyone working on this period 1880-1915 is blessed and overwhelmed by the great extent of the sources. I owe thanks to many of their custodians, notably the librarians of the Bodleian, the Victoria and Albert Museum and the Royal Institute of British Architects, but most especially to the exceptionally helpful and patient librarians of the Guildhall Library in the City of London, as well as to the Head Reference Librarian of Shoreditch, Mr. Robert Thompson, for much valuable advice on the very extensive collection of furniture books and periodicals at Shoreditch, and to the Reference Librarian, Miss Ailsa Watson.

For the generous number of illustrations far-sightedly demanded by the publishers I am indebted to:

The Victoria and Albert Museum, The Shire Museum, Leicester, Mr. G. Rolfe of E. Gomme Ltd., Janet Piper, Ivan Sparkes, Dr. Jonathan Wager, Clive Wainwright and Mr. K. Wootten and the Press Office of Liberty and Co.

But most of all to the Head Librarian of Shoreditch, Mr. T. Patston for permission to photograph many items in the library.

Many illustrations have been generously supplied by Sotheby's Belgravia; I wish to thank Christopher Payne for making these available and Arabella Douglas-Menzies for obtaining them.

For permission to incorporate extracts and illustrations I thank:

John Harris, Curator of the Drawings Collection of the R.I.B.A., *The Cabinet Maker, Country Life,* Hodder and Stoughton, David and Charles and *The Studio.*

I am grateful to Miss Christina George for converting copiously corrected manuscript into decent typescript, to Mrs. Cherry Lewis for seeing the book through the press with cheerful patience and Holmesian initiative, and lastly but most of all, to my husband for so many things.

For Peter, who has tolerated more stray
furniture than anyone should have to live with.

Contents

Pictorial Dictionary
of
British 19th Century
FURNITURE DESIGN

Introduction by Edward Joy

The nineteenth century produced more varied forms of furniture than any previous period in British history. Whereas about half a dozen names such as Chippendale, Hepplewhite, Adam and Sheraton dominated eighteenth century designs, the nineteenth century produced dozens of independent designers particularly towards the end of the period. As the furniture trade developed, so manufacturers and retailing split. Catalogues began to be used in retail shops as they are today. Competition between retailers and the use of the new design books, resulted in a large number of designs, not only new ones but also a constant looking backwards to earlier centuries for inspiration. This change in the structure of the industry made full use of highly individual interpretations of Gothic, Renaissance, Elizabethan, 'Naturalistic' styles, Egyptian, Old French, Louis Quatorze, Louis Quinze, and Italian decorations, all applied to a wide variety of furniture, and one can understand that the complexity of the subject is best explained by a very large number of illustrations. This is the reason why some 6,000 illustrations appear within this book. Other books so far written on the period have tended to concentrate almost entirely on the names of leading designers and pieces made for the few important exhibitions, which, while relevant to taste at the top end of the market, had little influence on the vast flow of furniture produced for the wealthy middle class market, the type of furniture that one finds today in market shops and at auctions.

The *Dictionary* is made up from forty-nine contemporary design and pattern books. Each piece of furniture has been sorted into its physical characteristics (e.g. table with three legs), so that it is only necessary to glance down the list of contents to identify into which category any particular piece belongs. This simple format has avoided the pitfalls of using contemporary nomenclature interlaced as it is with later fashionable terminology (dressoir and 'Glastonbury' chair). Within each category the pieces are arranged into chronological order so that the evolution of each type is clearly seen. This provides the first major study of the very wide range of furniture produced in this prolific century and should become the standard work of reference on this subject.

£25.00

ISBN 0 902028 47 2

An Antique Collectors' Club Research Project

Styles and Fashions

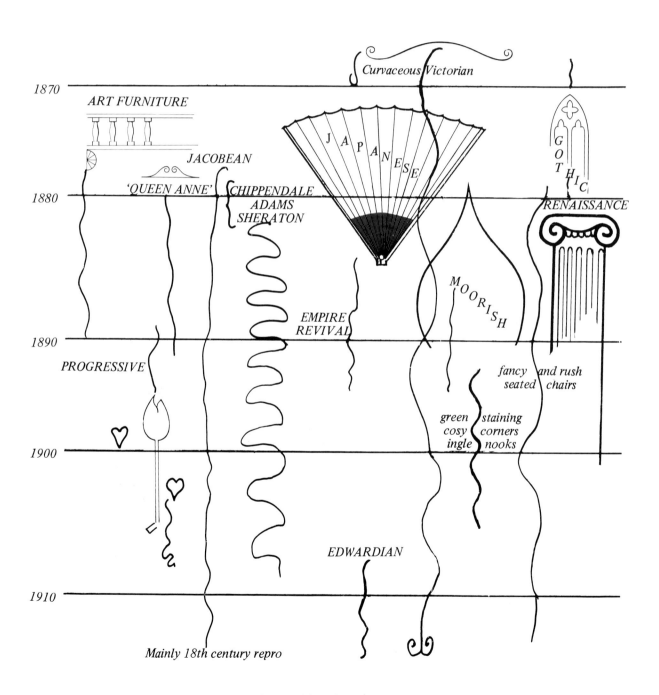

1870

ART FURNITURE

Curvaceous Victorian

JAPANESE

GOTHIC

JACOBEAN

1880

'QUEEN ANNE'   CHIPPENDALE
ADAMS
SHERATON

RENAISSANCE

MOORISH

EMPIRE
REVIVAL

1890

PROGRESSIVE

fancy and rush
seated chairs

green staining
cosy corners
ingle nooks

1900

EDWARDIAN

1910

Mainly 18th century repro

Formative Events and Influences

1867	Bruce Talbert's 'Gothic Forms'	Beginnings of long-lasting revival of English
1868	C.L. Eastlake's 'Hints on Household Taste'	18th century styles
1871	Collinson and Lock's 'Artistic Furniture' catalogue	Enthusiasm for 'Queen Anne' architecture and Japanese artefacts
	Collcutt's black, gold and painted cabinet	
1875	Liberty & Co. opened	
1876	Bruce Talbert's 'Ancient and Modern Furniture'	
1877	Watt's Godwin catalogue 'Art Furniture'	
1877-8	'Art in the Home' series	
1878	Paris Exhibition	
1880	Dresser's Art Furnishers Alliance	Books on Italian Renaissance
	'Cabinet Maker' magazine founded	
1881	Edis: Furniture and Decoration of Town Houses	
1882	Century Guild founded	Mechanisation increasing
1883	Jones Collection opened	
1884	'Healtheries' Exhibition	Mackmurdo's tall shafts and wide cornices
1885	'Inventories' Exhibition	
1886	'Shipperies' Exhibition	
1888	Arts and Crafts Exhibition Society founded, 1st Exhibition.	
1889	Arts and Crafts Exhibition	
1890	Kenton and Co.; Arts and Crafts Exhibition	
1893	'Studio' magazine founded; Arts and Crafts Exhibition	Tall 'quaint' chairs by Baldock
1896	Arts and Crafts Exhibition	J.S. Henry tall chairs at Amsterdam
1897	Diamond Jubilee; Baillie Scott Darmstadt furniture	Patriotic fervour; more factory production
1899	Arts and Crafts Exhibition	
1900	Paris Exhibition; Wallace Collection opened	
1901	Glasgow Exhibition	
1902	Turin Exhibition: Voysey's chair, Scottish Pavilion by Mackintosh	
	Mackintosh's furniture for Miss Cranston's tearooms	
1904	St. Louis Exhibition	British exhibits all reproductions
1905 onwards	Progressive killed by economic difficulties	Gimson and the Barnsleys start working in the Cotswolds
1906	Baillie Scott's 'Houses and Gardens'	
1912	Paul Poiret's painted Martine furniture	

A contrast of styles. Plate 1a, above, shows a gothic bed and wash-stand in carved, painted and gilt wood. Designed by William Burges for the guest chamber, Tower House, Melbury Road, London, 1880.

Plate 1e, right: brass bed with a progressive furniture tulip motif for decoration, c.1900.

CHAPTER 1

The Scene 1880-1915 and its Prehistory

The prosperity, resources and confidence generated by the industrial revolution and an ever-growing Empire produced the wide variety and middling taste of much late nineteenth century furniture. Whereas the interest of important eighteenth century furniture lies in its formality, elegance and suitability to the aristocratic way of life, the interest of much late nineteenth century production lies in its all-tastes, all-talents diversity and the fact that it was available, if not to all, certainly to vast numbers of people. It is mainly not great or 'important' in the auctioneer's narrow sense, but it does reflect the vigour and individualism of its time.

Plates 1a-1j show some of the diversity. The range was so unusually wide that the furniture trade in Britain in that third of a century from 1880 can usefully be thought of as a Grand Variety Performance. There were the popular acts: the traditional chairs like a chorus in the background and those old established favourites the curvaceous Victorian forms. The many pastiches of period styles provided olde-time music-hall acts whilst top quality reproductions, like classical performers, gave conscientious renderings of concert pieces. There were brash impersonators with crudely faked appearances and serious monologues by gothic items, before, lastly, the startling new acts which shocked and delighted by their simplicity and directness, shedding decoration and revealing structure.

Victoria's reign had opened in the midst of the 'battle of the styles' with so-called Grecian, gothic, Elizabethan, Italian Renaissance and French rococo vying for popularity. But often it was merely the decorative details of these styles applied to the same basic shapes. From the mid century the most generally accepted style was, undoubtedly, that based on the curve as in Plates 2-8, with the balloon back chairs, the serpentine fronted cabinets, the curl panels, the round and oval tables and the curvaceous seats and supports all with rounded off corners. The style, inspired initially by features of French rococo furniture and well served by the strength of mahogany, was influenced by the curvaceous shapes formed by the new sprung upholstery.

This 'reassuring rotundity' in mahogany dominated popular taste until the 1870s, seriously challenged only by the fashion for French furniture in drawing rooms and by the never more than minor appetite for supposedly 'gothic' designs. These, clothed with decorative features of medieval stonework, grew out of the religious and emotional gothic revivalism of Pugin and other architects amid the Tractarian and ritualist background of the 1840s and 1850s. Plate 14.

Plate 1b. Ormolu mounted parquetry occasional table stamped Edwards and Roberts. It is a copy of a table in the Jones Collection so was probably made after 1883 when the Collection opened.

No. 69.—£2.2.0.　　　No. 70.—£3.7.6.
Richly Carved Italian Chairs.

Plate 1c. Reproduction Italian Renaissance chairs in early twentieth century catalogue of Hamptons, Pall Mall.

Plate 1d. Ebonized and painted art furniture cabinet, 1880s.

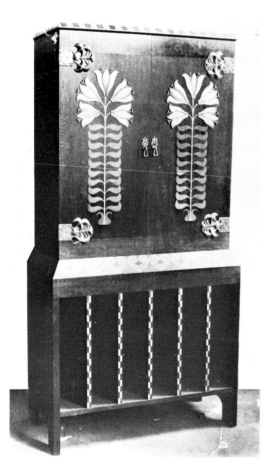

Plate 1f. Music cabinet designed by Baillie Scott, 1898.

Plate 1g. Chair and writing table designed by C.F.A. Voysey and exhibited Turin, 1902. Cabinet Maker, *March 1903.*

The thought and ferment inspiring gothic waned as the zeal for things ecclesiastical made way in the 1870s for the fervour of aestheticism and the 'new Reformed Faith in art'. This fostered 'art manufacturers' of all kinds including 'art furniture'. The challenge came also from the trade's excited rediscovery of the fine proportions and detail of English eighteenth century furniture and the making of many reproductions from that and earlier centuries.

There was too, the crusade for more honestly constructed, rational and purposeful furniture. This 'progressive' was the most significant and promising development in furniture at the end of the nineteenth century so its emergence deserves detailed investigation (Chapters 4 and 5). But, as it constituted only a fraction of the bulk of production, the other 'acts' must be considered first and these, including the mere repro, are surprisingly interesting because of the energetic debate and attention and strong views that lay behind and moulded the taste for them. It was a time when not only "crotchety, cracked young men" were expected to care about the shapes of their possessions; and it is because it is possible, via the literature, magazines, comic opera, song covers and posters of the time, to re-enter that atmosphere, that some of the furniture can be so enjoyably and amusingly evocative to live with. To choose a decade and furnish a period room of the 70s, 80s or 90s would be a challenging and entertaining project.

After having studied the rest of the scene, the prehistory and emergence of the simpler 'progressive' furniture (Plates 1f, g, h and 101-186) should reveal itself more clearly. At its best it achieved a new sophisticated simplicity without austerity and offered creative possibilities which have never been fully explored.

This is one of the first periods in furniture history for which there are overwhelming written sources. Many students will need to become addicted to reading the *Cabinet Maker* and *Furniture Gazette,* the reports of contemporaries, the advertisements and catalogues of firms and their archives before a full history and understanding of the period can emerge. This is only a preliminary study. Much of it consists of quotations from contemporary sources to provide evidence for the framework set up but some of the outline will inevitably shift after further investigation.

This is one of the attractions of the period for enquiring collectors. By finding items and investigating their provenance they can actively help to fill in the picture. Pieces with makers' labels are to be found and firms' catalogues do turn up in attics and jumble sales.

One of the reasons for writing now about the period 1880-1915 is that much of the best of it remains to be discovered. Energetic collectors and furnishers can hope – and expect – to find quality pieces which are as yet disregarded as merely old stuff with only second-hand value.

What can be more tempting than that?

But there is little time. If the desperately short sighted wholesale shipping abroad of our furniture heritage is allowed to continue it will soon be too late.

Plate 1h. Chair with high inlaid back, flat arms and triple stretchers characteristic of 1895-1905.

Plate 1j. Settee designed by Christopher Dresser, c.1880.

CHAPTER 2

Continuing Victorian Forms

Plate 2a. Curvaceous walnut, buttoned lady's/ gentleman's chair with free-standing scrolled arms and low cabriole legs.
Courtesy Sotheby's Belgravia.

This period, 1880 onwards, illustrates a strand in furniture history that, although discerned in earlier periods, has been difficult to illustrate because of the lack of printed sources. But catalogues of this era clearly demonstrate how long popular forms may continue to be produced even after they have ceased to be fashionable.

This chapter might well be sub-titled: 'It's later than you think', as many forms, such as the balloon back and various upholstered chairs, the curved mouldings and curvaceous outlines of sideboards, chiffoniers, cabinets and wash-stands which evolved early in Victoria's reign continued to be made until the end of the century though, of course, they were by then no longer fashionable. Plate 4 shows advertisements of the 1890s of forms which had been popular for half a century. Peter Floud, that pioneer of Victorian studies, brilliantly summarised the characteristics of this Victorian style[1] (Plates 2-8) as: "... the rounding off of all corners and the elimination of all angularities and surface irregularities" and "the tendency to merge the separate parts of each piece of furniture into a unified, undifferentiated whole. Arms and backs of sofas are joined together in a single enveloping semi-circle. The distinction between pedestal and base in the standard Regency loo table is obliterated." There is a ubiquitous "heavy handed curve which almost gives the wood the appearance of having been squeezed from a tube" – moulded rather than carved. Plate 6.

P. Thomson's *Cabinet Maker's Assistant* published in 1853 most clearly portrays this curvaceous Victorian rococo style and points out that smooth, curved surfaces best show off the brilliant colours and high polish of mahogany. Plate 7.

Plate 2b. Elaborately carved balloon back chair with 'hump'.

Plate 3. Walnut framed settee with concave-curved seat, low cabriole legs and flower carved crest. Note the continuous curve of arms and back. Mid-nineteenth century.
Courtesy Sotheby's Belgravia.

Stained Mahogany Chair, covered in American Cloth ..   .. 4/11 and 8/6
Library or Smoking Chairs, covered in Roan Leather   ..   ..   .. 65/0 to 100/0
   Do.   do.   superior, all hair ..   .. 84/0 ,, 170/0

The "Sutherland."   *The "Jersey."*

LADIES' "SUTHERLAND" EASY, in Cretonne   ..   .. 28/6 and 35/0
GENTS'   do.   do.   do.   ..   .. 35/0 ,, 45/0
"JERSEY" EASY, in Cretonne, very comfortable   ..   .. 37/6 to 112/6
   Do.   do.   in Saddle Bags and Velvet   ..   .. 63/0 ,, 170/0
   Do.   do.   in Saddle Bags and Velvet, bolster top, stuffed hair, 80/0 ,, 190/0

All the above are delivered Carriage Free, subject to the Conditions set forth on page 1427

Plate 4. From Harrods 1895 catalogue. All these items came into vogue before the middle of the century.
Courtesy David and Charles, from their facsimile reprint Victorian Shopping.

Plate 5a, left: Davenport with several curves and a keyboard lid. Second half nineteenth century. Plate 5b, above: English walnut marquetry side cabinet with serpentine outline. The central door is inlaid with fruitwood scroll work. 5ft. 1in. wide. Possibly c.1860 but this type continued to be made until the end of the century.
Courtesy Sotheby's Belgravia.

Plate 6. Walnut dining table with quatrefoil shaped top of dark and lighter contrasting woods. United pedestal and base offer a good example of the curvaceous Victorian style, c.1860.
Courtesy Victoria and Albert Museum.

Plate 7. Slab sideboard and cabinet from Thomson's (Blackie's) Cabinet Maker's Assistant, 1853.

Plate 8. Suite of nine comprising couch, lady's and gentleman's chairs and six singles with walnut frames and finished in Rep. £5−£15 according to quality. From Furniture Trade Catalogue, 1882.

Plates 8, 9 and 10 illustrate items from the *Furniture Trade Catalogue* of 1882. Most of them had appeared in the 1840s or 50s in Smee's catalogue or Hindley's Order Book[2] or the *Cabinet Maker's Assistant*. Presumably these forms lasted so long because they were so acceptably comfortable or convenient. Mr. Pickwick's "substantial comfort" was a prime requirement in Victorian homes.[3] Another factor fostering this conservatism may have been the dearth of new pattern books in the middle of the century, as this forced the trade to rely considerably on reprints. Loudon's *Encyclopaedia*,[4] with its pre-1833 furniture, went into eleven editions up to 1867 and Thomas King's *Modern Style of Cabinet Work*, 1829, was reissued, unaltered, as late as 1862. Although many diverse forms had been seen in exhibitions, most of them were too elaborate to have much influence on modest domestic furniture.

LATER FEATURES

Some of the continuing forms developed characteristics by which they can be recognised as later products. Late balloon backs often had

280   281   282

Plate 9. Loo table, octagonal centre table and chairs from Furniture Trade Catalogue, *1882. All had been popular since the middle of the century.*

Plate 10. Walnut inlaid chiffonier with mirror back, glass doors and marble top, 4ft. wide, £5 5s.–£7. Matching dressing table and washstand £22–£30. All from Furniture Trade Catalogue, *1882.*

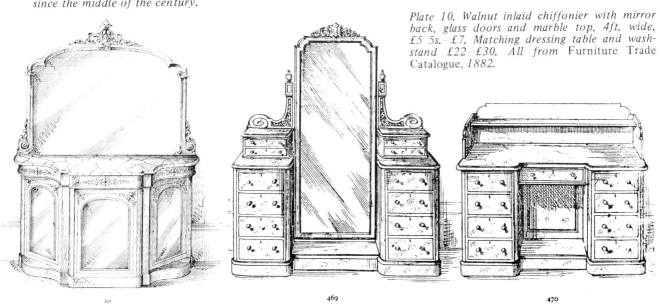

350   469   470

fussier outlines, as in Plate 11, and were clumsier. The dot and dash grooving as on that chair was illustrated in Thomson's *Cabinet Maker* but seems to be common only later. The low back chairs which had come into fashion in the 1840s with back and arms forming a continuous upholstered semi-circle supported only in the middle, came to have a supporting row of turned spindles from the late 60s onwards. Early forms decorated with incised lines are almost certainly post-1870 as are ebonized pieces and those stained green. Many late loo tables were oval and the more richly inlaid the later they are likely to be.

The nature of the carving is often the surest guide to dating. "Whereas 1840s and 50s balloon backs, chiffoniers, etc. in the rococo taste are carved with confidence, having an assured line which swings in a flowing way and is never given to abrupt endings, later pieces have lost that flow and have uneasy cranks to the scrolls".[5] Good early carving finishes relevantly within its allotted boundaries whilst the later often ends carelessly as, for example, on the console brackets of bookcases. At the end of the century there was "much sunken carving against a ground which is usually unattractive as the figure of the wood remains undeveloped."

As for the wood itself, early work was often in magnificent mahogany and rosewood whilst veneers, of seat rails for example, were up to a quarter of an inch thick. By the end of the century, prices had risen and wood was used more sparingly; and as the style ceased to be high fashion cheaper varieties were utilised.

It is necessary to stress that although this curvaceous style was still available at the end of the century, it was no longer fashionable then. Even in 1882 a critic was writing: "It seems hardly possible to believe that less than twenty years ago mahogany serpentine fronted sideboards with curl panels were preferred before the solid and straight article".[6]

REVIVALIST GOTHIC

The other essentially Victorian style which lingered on for the rest of the reign was the 'modern English' or 'High Victorian' gothic more relevantly named 'revivalist gothic' because it was the product of the enthusiasm of gothic revivalist architects like A.W.N. Pugin who crusaded with immense seriousness and ardour for that 'pointed style' as the only "acceptable, truthful" form. Unfortunately, as little medieval gothic furniture survived, and that little did not provide prototypes to meet Victorian needs for sideboards, whatnots, tea tables and china cabinets, etc., designers had to invent structured shapes and then clothe them with chamfering, cusping, crockets, columns, roundels, foliage, gables and other features derived from gothic stonework. Plates 12-21. Thomson's *Cabinet Maker's Assistant,* 1853, had given very little space to gothic designs but did explain the popularity of oak: "As the Gothic style is rather stern and angular, depending much for its effect on bold light and shadow, oak, walnut and our home grown furniture woods in general are better suited to it than mahogany".

It is difficult to date revivalist gothic and difficult to guess how much of it was made after 1880. It may help to remember that Hollands and Gillows had made a good deal of it for the House of Lords from the 1840s when Pugin designed it, and that a version inspired by fifteenth century perpendicular architecture had received much publicity from Pugin's Medieval Court at the Great Exhibition.

But it was the sterner, more obviously structural thirteenth century gothic as seen in the great bookcase (Plate 12) designed in 1862 by the

Plate 11. Later balloon back chair with dot-dash grooving.

24

Plate 12. Very tall bookcase with stump columns, gables, cusping and other features of gothic stonework and revealed construction. Designed by the architect Norman Shaw and shown at the 1862 Exhibition. It was this type of gothic which influenced commercial production until the 1880s.
Courtesy Victoria and Albert Museum.

Plate 15. Gothic dressoir, designed by Bruce Talbert and made by Holland and Sons in the 1870s and 1880s.
Courtesy Victoria and Albert Museum.

Plate 13. Oak gothic table with carved and chamfered decoration, designed by Pugin about 1851. Here cusping and ogee forms are used with originality. Courtesy Victoria and Albert Museum.

architect Norman Shaw, that came to influence commercial production. Another architect William Burges was a very energetic campaigner for this earlier gothic manner (Plate 1a).[7] Some of the most attractive of the new gothic was that designed in 1865 by Charles Bevan for the West Riding industrialist Titus Salt, jun. This was illustrated in *Furniture History,* Volume III, 1967, and is now, fortunately, housed at Lotherton Hall, a Leeds City Museum.

It was probably not until the late 60s that much commercial gothic was available. Then and in the 70s geometrical inlay was the rage, "the stop chamfer was a symbol of artistic salvation", Hollands were producing vast dressoirs as in Plate 15 and Cox and Sims offered ecclesiastical and domestic items as in Plate 16. These were deemed "the right sort of thing for the elite."

Some of this furniture, like Plate 14, clearly evokes the uncompromising idealism and missionary zeal of the Oxford movement-ish gothic revivalists. As Charles Handley Read noted, the enthusiasm of those who believed in gothic as the only possible style shows in "their passionate exaggeration, neither pedantic, nor tepid but zealous". Some gothic is more simply bold and confident (Plates 17a and 17b) and this is probably later; but much of it merely had dully repetitive features to conform in 'gothic' buildings (Plate 18).

When Hollands exhibited the Plate 15 dressoir again in 1881, *The Builder* commented that it was of a type going out of favour and in October 1886 *The Cabinet Maker* noted that "the Gothic furniture which Welby Pugin endeavoured to foist upon the public now sells for a song."

It was plainer Bevan-like designs which lingered on and simple forms as in Plate 21 of 'Medieval Bed Chamber Furniture' which Shoolbred illustrated in their catalogue from 1874-89. It is interesting and surprising to find the very independent minded Christopher Dresser offering several gothic designs, Plates 19 and 20, when he became editor of the *Furniture Gazette* in 1880. He presumably felt the style still had appeal and a future.

Plate 14. Rampant, ideological gothic overtakes this 1ft. 10in. wide desk in pine. Courtesy Sotheby's Belgravia.

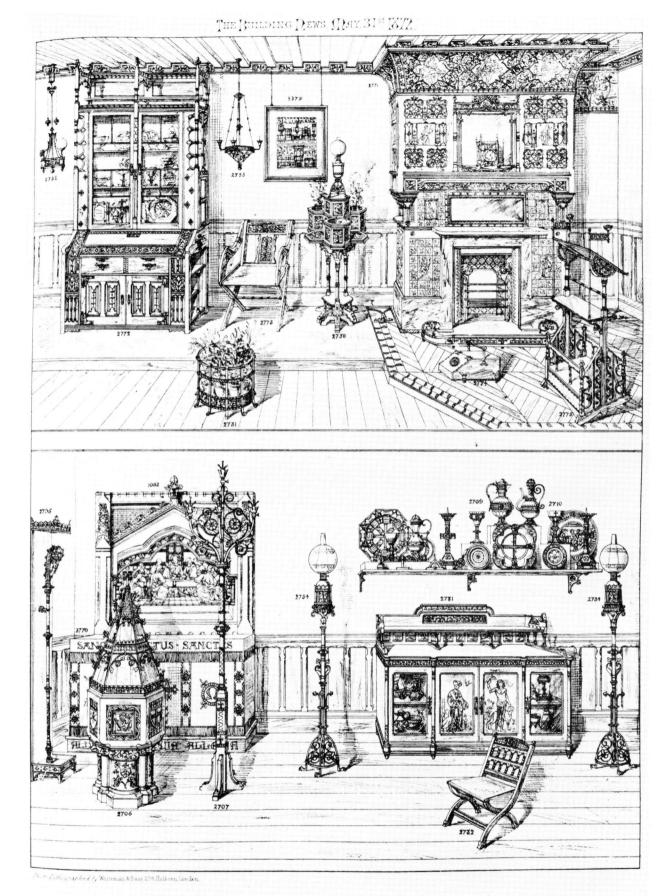

INTERNATIONAL + EXHIBITION + 1872. MESSRS + COX + & + SONS + EXHIBITS.

Plate 16. Ecclesiastical and domestic furniture exhibited at 1872 Exhibition by Cox and Sons. Building News, *May 31, 1872.*

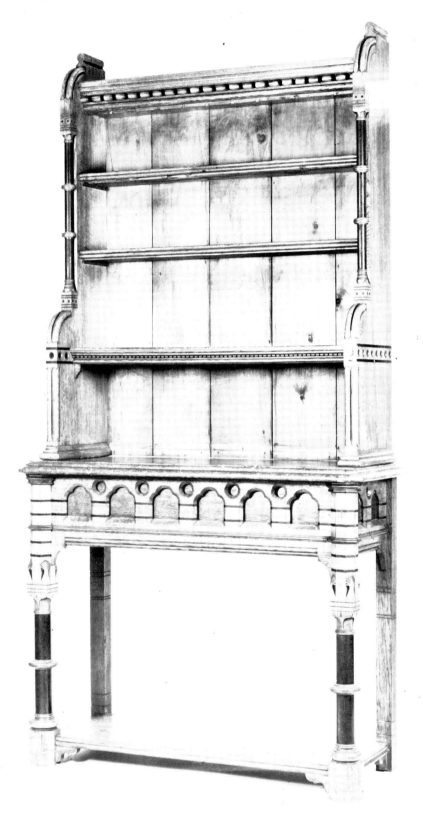

Plate 17a. Bold revivalist gothic bookcase in oak and ebony.
Courtesy Sotheby's Belgravia.

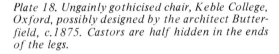

Plate 17b. Vigorous revivalist gothic oak sideboard, c.1880.
Courtesy Sotheby's Belgravia.

Plate 18. Ungainly gothicised chair, Keble College, Oxford, possibly designed by the architect Butterfield, c.1875. Castors are half hidden in the ends of the legs.

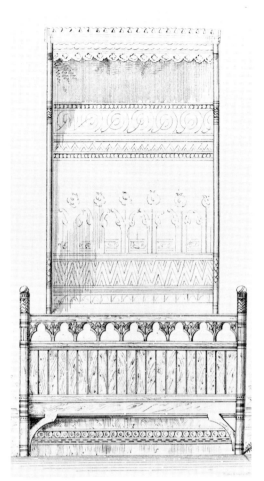

Plate 19. 'Bedstead in gothic style' possibly designed by Christopher Dresser, Furniture Gazette, *1880.*

But the designer H.W. Batley[8] wrote in 1882: "The Gothic revival of some years back, although very sound and good in its way, was soon found to be too heavy and severe for domestic use . . ." So it seems that although gothic was present throughout the reign its commercial domestic heyday lasted less than a couple of decades. Its natural successor was the furniture of Bruce Talbert (Chapter 4) which can be seen as a kind of secularised gothic: honest construction but without crockets, cusps or corbels.

Only an intensive search in the order books of such firms as Gillow and Holland will reveal how much revivalist gothic was made in the last two decades of the century. Comyn Ching of Long Acre, it may be noted, was still advertising 'a large and varied stock of medieval cabinet handles' in the later 1880s.

OTHER CONTINUING FORMS

Other items which continued to be produced throughout the reign

Plate 22, right. The display card of Edwin Skull, c.1865-70. Many of these designs continued to be available up to 1915.
Courtesy High Wycombe Public Library.

EDWIN SKULL,

SKULL'S PATENT PLECTANEUM CHAIR·
IN AMERICAN BIRCH.

EDWIN SKULL,
Manufacturer
OF EVERY DESCRIPTION OF CHAIRS
HIGH WYCOMBE,
BUCKS.

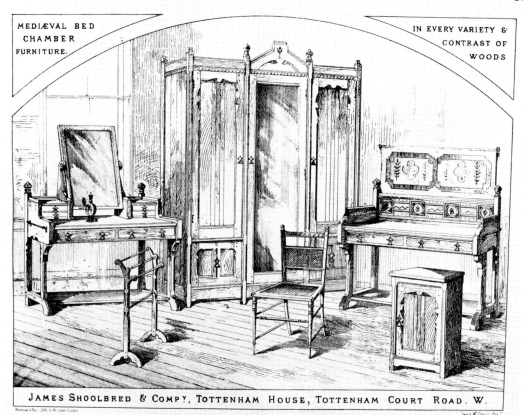

MEDIÆVAL BED CHAMBER FURNITURE.

IN EVERY VARIETY & CONTRAST OF WOODS

JAMES SHOOLBRED & COMP?, TOTTENHAM HOUSE, TOTTENHAM COURT ROAD. W.

Plate 21. 'Medieval (gothic) Bed Chamber Furniture' appeared in Shoolbred's catalogues at least from 1874-89.

Plate 20. 'Wardrobes in the gothic style' possibly designed by Christopher Dresser, Furniture Gazette, *1880.*

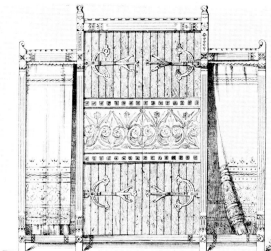

were various Windsor chairs. Plate 22 shows the great variety of Windsors on the trade card of Edwin Skull of High Wycombe in the 1870s. Most were of old established patterns and many were still available up to 1915. Traditional chair making continued to be carried on up and down the country until it succumbed to the too competitive prices of the highly organised Wycombe trade, or local factory production, or bentwood imports around 1900.

The 'French' furniture which was popular for most of the reign is more fittingly discussed in the next chapter on fashionable reproductions.

Footnotes

1. Connoisseur Period Guides: *The Early Victorian Period*, pp.35-50.
2. Smee in Victoria and Albert Library, Hindley in Marylebone Public Library.
3. John Gloag, *Victorian Comfort, a social history of design 1830-1900.*
4. J.C. Loudon, *Encyclopaedia of Cottage, Farmhouse and Villa Architecture and Furniture,* 1833.
5. I am indebted to Dr Penelope Eames for these perceptive comments.
6. *Cabinet Maker*, Vol. 3, p.75, October 2, 1882.
7. *Building News,* Vol. 14, p.260, April 12, 1867, quotes J. Beavington Atkinson: Gothic Furniture in *Art Journal*, 1867. He notes of William Burges: "This well known architect has played a prominent part in the revived art manufacturers after the Gothic style."
8. Preface to his *A series of studies for domestic furniture and decoration.*

CHAPTER 3

Fashionable Reproduction Furniture 1880 ˜ 1915

But the continuing popularity of the curvaceous and other early Victorian forms and the waning taste for watered down revivalist gothic were not the main features of the fashionable furniture scene from 1880. There was a burgeoning functionist trend which will be discussed in Chapter 5; but this third of a century was rather the great heyday of the attempted reproductions of the modes of other times and other lands. A wander round the windows of the West End of London in the 1880s would have provided a bizarre world furniture exhibition – like the Finale of the Grand Variety Performance with all the actors on the stage together. Examples ranged from the cheap and nasty, miserably proportioned repro pieces with stuck-on mouldings and poorly carved detail, to conscientious reproductions of the highest quality and craftsmanship and to some original pieces fashioned from traditional elements. Some are worth cherishing for their quality and some because they are characteristic of a particular stage in the meanderings of taste.

The outline of the story is that throughout this period curvilinear rococo and later neo-classical French styles, often with ormolu mounts, were most fashionable for drawing rooms, with some items, especially tables and cabinets, inspired by French and Italian Renaissance forms. Dining rooms also might have a Renaissance flavour, but much Jacobean and some Elizabethan were greatly in favour there; whilst gothic, not greatly loved, might appear in halls and libraries. But for all rooms there was a great deal of what was imaginatively termed 'Queen Anne', 'Chippendale', 'Hepplewhite' and 'Sheraton'. Knowledge of furniture history was rudimentary and confused so these terms were often misapplied. Mrs. Haweis, one of the arbiters of taste, illustrated the confusion with her story: "Only the other day I was shown a French mirror (Louis XIV) by some really cultivated folks as: 'Queen Anne – Empire you know – genuine Chippendale'."

In only the second issue of the *Cabinet Maker* in 1880, the editor was in the midst of a controversy as to whether the rage for 'Queen Anne' was over and the *avant-garde* designer Christopher Dresser complained: "We are at present busying ourselves with the production of Chippendale, Queen Anne and Adam furniture although it is generally known that most of it is bad in structure and neither beautiful, dignified or picturesque in character".[1] The surfeit of repro was already so overwhelming that in November 1881 *The Artist and Journal of Home Culture* felt bound to ask: "Are we to be forever

Plate 23. Cabinet on stand – one of the many reproduction pieces of the period.

looking backward? Is there no power of primary design left amongst us, but only a faculty for the new combination of bits of our ancestors' work? . . . it may be enquired whether we do not get a great deal more archaeology than is good for us?"

They surely did. For the next third of a century the widely circulated magazines the *Cabinet Maker* and the *Furniture Gazette* and a host of books provided plates of designs in the medieval or gothic, the Renaissance, Tudor, Jacobean or Old English, Queen Anne, Chippendale, Hepplewhite, Sheraton, Louis XIV, XV, XVI and Empire, Moresque and Anglo-Japanese modes. Before considering what each offered it is useful to try to understand the contemporary attitude to reproductions.

Since Victoria's accession in 1837 the population of England and Wales had increased by two thirds to nearly 25 million and it is usually assumed that the rapidly growing, up and coming, middling sections of society, not too sure of their status, were anxious to furnish in conservative and acceptable styles. But why were reproductions so respectably acceptable? There must be many explanations, but one of the more forceful pressures must surely have been the backlog, the mound of information, interest and liking generated by decades of exhibitions since that of 1851. People had been trained by the persuasive publicity of these to look back at the creations of other times and places. Undoubtedly many wished to own them; the hunt for old furniture was in full cry. But as A. Jonquet, a designer, remarked of genuine antiques in 1877, "The scarcity and great cost of such works places them beyond the reach of all but wealthy collectors "[2] and the *Cabinet Maker* vouched ". . . if originals are not obtainable reproductions sell equally well."

So the Trade made, and the public accepted, repros of what was deemed right and fitting from 'old England's past' and the *ancien régime.* When in 1882 William Whiteley, pioneering a new form of publicity, showed a completely 'fitted up' Chippendale dining room in

Plate 24a. Louis XV style settee made by Hindley and Wilkinson, Old Bond Street, early twentieth century. Tapestries for upholstery were specially woven for them in Aubusson. They claimed "the beauty and charm of the original tapestries is marvellously retained even to the faded and subtle tints which time has given to the old pieces."

Plate 24b. The armchair on the left is en suite *with the settee in Plate 24a. That on the right shows a most effective and comparatively inexpensive treatment in the upholstering of the same model covered in a rich silk damask with embroidered appliqué border or framework following the contour of the back and seat. Hindley and Wilkinson catalogue between 1900-1912.*

Plate 25. Louis XVI style gilt settee and chairs. Hindley and Wilkinson catalogue between 1900-1912.

one of the windows in his Queen's Road store, the *Cabinet Maker* rejoiced: "In looking at such a picture in its entirety it is easy to understand how that period of our national furniture history has taken such a hold upon society of late. It is so homely, unaffected and thoroughly national."[3] Rather surprisingly, repro was not inevitably derided as escapism even by the progressive. When, for example, Mr. and Mrs. J.S. Beale commissioned the forward looking architect Phillip Webb to design a country property for them at Standen in 1890, they did not order much advanced furniture but rather good quality eighteenth century repro from S. and H. Jewell and some plain traditional pieces from Morris & Co.

THE MAIN REPRODUCTION STYLES

FRENCH

Louis XV and Louis XVI

The elegant twistings of the C scrolled, rococo Louis Quinze were high fashion for drawing rooms and boudoirs from before 1840 until well into the twentieth century. The Louis Seize too came into favour from around 1855 when Jackson and Graham won a Gold Medal at the Paris Exhibition for a satin wood, ormolu mounted, marquetry cabinet inspired by that style. Queen Victoria too, must have fostered the fashion by buying a Louis XVI style table and cabinet at that exhibition.

In the mid-century there was general agreement as to the superiority of French cabinet making and design so, presumably, a good deal was imported. How early British firms were themselves producing good quality 'French' pieces is not clear, but many were exhibiting them at the 1862 Exhibition. Certainly the high quality firm of Wright and Mansfield (1860s-86) "made a point of giving special attention to the French style, Louis Seize in particular."[4] Among other quality firms, Holland and Sons and Jackson and Graham, who frequently employed French workers, offered plenty of choice. James Shoolbred and Co. illustrated Louis Seize in their catalogues from 1874-89.

Plates 24-26 show particularly fine craftsmanship from Hindley and Wilkinson who, early in the twentieth century, had "a superb stock of

Plate 26. Mistakenly described as a Louis XIV commode this is another high quality reproduction of Louis XV style by Hindley and Wilkinson, 1900-1912 catalogue.

French cabinet work of the best periods ... copied from the French Museums and other collections."[5]

Gillows devoted twenty seven pages of their 1908 catalogue to French furniture and obviously took its production very seriously claiming: "Our Exhibition of French furniture is not surpassed even in Paris and is the result of many years search through Museums and Private Collections for the finest models and the means of reproducing them ... The work is carried out in Paris, either at our own Factory or by *ébénistes* of the highest reputation with whom we enjoy the closest relations."

But the cost was high. Even in 1881 it was reported[6] that "it was, indeed, the cost of the cabinet work of the latter [Louis XVI] period which has driven manufacturers to reproduce the sideboards, cabinets, chairs and tables of the Stuart or Flemish styles."

But trade in reproductions of French items must have been stimulated by the opening in 1883 of the magnificent Jones Collection of French furniture at the South Kensington Museum (as the V & A was then known) and received a further boost when the Wallace Collection opened in 1900.

Further details of high quality reproductions of French furniture will be found in Chapter 7.

But a good deal of work in the French styles was in the feeble over-decorated mishmash known in the trade as Lewy Quinzy or Louis the Hotel and often badly let down by poor quality 'ormolulu' mounts.

The Empire Revival: 1880s and 1890s

Empire furniture of the Napoleonic era was the least copied of the French styles but there was a distinct if limited revival in the 1880s and 90s. An editorial in the *Cabinet Maker* of May 1st, 1884 may have triggered it off or may itself have been sparked off by a few items of Empire form already made by some quality firm, or perhaps by some items of Napoleon's own furniture then permanently on view at Madame Tussaud's in Baker Street. The editor suggested "Anglo-Japanese, Anglo-Moresque and other fancies have had a good innings and without any desire to bowl them out I think that some success might be scored by a new departure ... it did occur to me the other day that there was a modern French epoch which had not received at the hands of our trade designers the attention which it deserves. I refer to the 'Empire' style."

Plate 27. *Sketches of Empire Revival furniture made by Robert Christie for Mr. Alexander Henderson of Buscot, 1891.* Cabinet Maker.

Plate 28. *Marble topped, Empire type mahogany side table inlaid with brass, stamped Edwards and Roberts. Adapted from a design by Percier and Fontaine, probably made in the 1890s during the Empire Revival.*
Courtesy Victoria and Albert Museum.

Plate 29. Cabinet with fine inlays exhibited by Jackson and Graham at the 1878 Exhibition. Less elaborate than the 'Juno'.

The following August an upholstered Empire type chair by M.A. Harper & Son was illustrated in the magazine but there is no evidence to suggest a rush into Empire forms. Robert Brook included Empire in his *Elements of Styles in Furniture and Woodwork* in 1889 but in September 1891 the *Cabinet Maker* complained "I have drawn attention to the Empire style as offering possibilities . . . but a very few on this side of the Channel have had the courage to tackle it except in a 'bitty' way."

But that year "the purchaser of the Burne-Jones sequence of 'Briar Rose' paintings asked Mr. Christie to furnish some Empire rooms."[7] This was Mr. Alexander Henderson of Buscot Park and it was presumably the very high quality writing table, chairs, etc. now at Buscot that were supplied by Mr. Robert Christie of 102 George Street, Portman Square, Plate 27. This Empire phase, incidentally, was paralleled in clothes in 1892 when Parisian modistes announced: "The Fashion for the following season is Empire."

Plate 28 shows an Empire table bearing the label of Edwards and Roberts, the Wardour Street firm who are known to have specialised in French styles including Empire. This and the Buscot pieces show the high level of craftsmanship available then.

There must have been some enthusiasm for this new departure because the *Cabinet Maker* in January 1895 referred to "Hope's Empire, this now popular style", and in October 1895 "now that this style is again to the fore", but in August 1895 the editor had lamented that ". . . whilst we (G.B.) have been toying with the Empire style, producing just a few choice though costly specimens U.S. makers had filled their showrooms with it." Certainly very, very few examples have been found in the Gillow sketch books.

Probably the Empire revival did not last much more than a decade.

RENAISSANCE

The interest in Italian painting of the Renaissance generated by the first great Art Treasures Exhibition of 1857 and already well served by art historians, was fanned in the 70s by the publication of J.A. Symonds' *Renaissance in Italy* and Walter Pater's *Studies in the History of the Renaissance*. Just as the middle third of the century had enjoyed a vision of an idealised Middle Ages so the last quarter relished a concept of an idealised Renaissance. These cultural associations and the architectural Renaissance revival fostered the appeal of Renaissance furniture.

Since the mid-century many features of Italian and French fifteenth and sixteenth century Renaissance and Mannerist work had been incorporated into exhibition pieces and quality furniture. These consisted of architectural forms such as pilasters and pediments, sculptural figures of classical gods, caryatids, grotesques, masks and animal supports and, thirdly, elaborate inlays of woods, stones, metals and ivory, variously known as intarsia and certosino work.

The post-1880 'Renaissance' work employed much of this decorative vocabulary and there was particular enthusiasm for inlaid work. It was said of Bruce Talbert's 'Juno' cabinet made by Jackson and Graham and sold for £2,000 at the Paris Exhibition of 1878, ". . . the inlays are in many cases so fine as to present the appearance of delicate pencilled work: and to crown the whole the workmanship is so perfect that even with the aid of a powerful magnifying glass scarcely the slightest

Plate 30. Occasional table with ivory intarsia work designed by Stephen Webb, late nineteenth century.
Courtesy Victoria and Albert Museum.

A DINING-ROOM, ADAPTED FROM THE FRENCH RENAISSANCE.

Plate 31. Dining room in the French Renaissance manner in the early twentieth century catalogue of Hampton and Sons, Pall Mall.

imperfection is to be found anywhere. In addition to the inlaying, some of which is solid, much of the ivory is engraved in the most delicate manner".[8] Plate 29. Gillows were commended in 1881 for some beautiful Italian cabinets of certosa work richly inlaid with ivory. The great exponent of these intarsia, inlay techniques was Stephen Webb. Plate 30.

G.J. Oakshott's *Details and Ornaments of the Renaissance*, 1888, with its carefully drawn decorated panels and intarsia designs must have been very useful to the trade.

But there was more robust 'Renaissance' work too as in Plate 31. The 'Renaissance' cabinet in Plate 32 "illustrates a type of work much used by Messrs. Hindley and Wilkinson in its application to heavy furniture and is specially suited to the furnishing of Halls, Dining Rooms and Billiard rooms" claims their catalogue[9] and suggests that the heavy chairs in Plate 33 are "specially suited for the furnishing of Halls and Dining Rooms in the style of the Italian or French Renaissance or are equally appropriate in Old English rooms of the Elizabethan or Stuart periods."

Plate 34 shows a mass market Flemish Renaissance table which appeared in the catalogue of Sewell and Sewell of London Wall about 1900 priced £3 12s.

40

Plate 32. Renaissance buffet with emblazoned arms in the panels, by Hindley and Wilkinson, catalogue 1900-1912.

Plate 34. Mass market Flemish Renaissance type table in catalogue of Sewell and Sewell, London Wall, c.1900, price £3 12s.

Plate 33. Hindley and Wilkinson state: "These chairs are perfect reproductions from old models and in every respect have the appearance of age. They are specially suited for the furnishing of Halls and Dining Rooms in the style of the Italian or French Renaissance: or . . . of the Elizabethan or Stuart periods," catalogue 1900-1912.

Plate 35. *Cabinet decorated with Renaissance features, late nineteenth century.*

Plate 36. *The fact that this Charles II chair was thought in 1885 to have belonged to Shakespeare illustrates the confused understanding of furniture history late in the nineteenth century.*

ELIZABETHAN

A mixture of sixteenth and seventeenth century features thought to be Elizabethan had been popular since the 1830s and although it was not one of the most popular styles after 1880, it appeared in many catalogues and was specially favoured for billiard rooms and some dining rooms. Peter Floud explained its earlier attraction very penetratingly: "It was indisputably British; it was rich without being vulgar and its coarse vigour did not overtax the somewhat limited finesse of the average British carver. Moreover its romantic and baronial associations were, of course, entirely in keeping with current literary preoccupations."

Libertys offered it in most of their catalogues. They advertised a late Elizabethan four post bed at £90 in their *Reproductions of Old English Furniture*, 1911.

The confused understanding of this style is well illustrated by the caption given in June 1885 to the late seventeenth century cane seated chair with near cabriole front legs in Plate 36: "It is very similar to most of the chairs which were in fashion during the reign of Elizabeth and for the rest of her century." Whilst the easy credulity of the 80s is shown by these galloping assumptions about that chair ". . . for long years cared for by Lady Barnard . . . and was brought by her from New Place, Stratford-on-Avon. Thus there is little doubt that it belonged to Shakespeare".

Plate 37. Reproductions c.1900 of Charles II type chairs with improbable designs in the backs.

JACOBEAN OR 'STUART'

The so-called 'Jacobean', embracing early and later seventeenth century features, was one of the most popular styles in the 1880s, especially for dining rooms. The *Cabinet Maker* of November 1st, 1880 credited Gillows with "... taking the lead in Jacobean, as they did years ago, their productions in that style mark an epoch in the furniture history of the country". The term came to imply genuine seventeenth century features, misunderstandings of them and also the reinterpreted gothic of Bruce Talbert (see Chapter 4) which in the 1870s and 80s was known as Jacobean or 'Early English'. Bulbous legged tables, court cupboards, panel back chairs and cane seated high backed chairs were all much reproduced. Plates 37 and 39. Libertys even devoted a whole catalogue to panel backs c.1910-11. Hamptons advertised 'Jacobean' for years in *The Studio,* for example, their 'Caroline Armchair accurately reproduced' in November 1901. 'Jacobean' inspired much good quality if dull furniture for several decades. The repro Jacobean

Plate 39. Seventeenth century type court cupboard illustrated in Wainwright's book. They traded in reproductions but some of their photographs appear to be of genuine items which they copied. 5ft. wide, 4ft. 6in. high, 1ft. 7in. deep. Originally £35, later £55.

Plate 40. Carved oak four post bed by Wainwrights. 7ft. high, 4ft. wide, 5ft. 6in. long, £75

Plate 38. William and Mary type chairs made by Wainwrights (?Hoxton N.1.?), c.1900, "finished in silver gilt colour cleverly antiqued with reddish ground colours, showing where silver has been rubbed off. Originally £15, later £23 5s. Note the back legs should be turned as in Plate 36 not, as here, like the front. From Wainwright stock book.

does not constitute an exciting collecting alley but the best of it is of fine quality and craftsmanship. Plate 41, The 'Bulwer', is a near reproduction of what was mistakenly thought to be a Cromwellian type of chair.[10]

EIGHTEENTH CENTURY ENGLISH STYLES

Eighteenth century English styles had been derided and sent upstairs to servants' rooms for a good half century. Their revival is largely credited to Wright and Mansfield who, according to the *Cabinet Maker*[11] "must be accounted the leaders of that pleasing fashion which has happily brought back into our houses, many of the charming shapes of the renowned eighteenth century cabinet makers. The best forms of Chippendale, Hepplewhite and particularly Sheraton have been made to live again under the renovating influence of these able manufacturers."

They exhibited a dwarf bookcase and a cabinet with eighteenth century neo-classical detail at the 1862 Exhibition in London and won great acclaim for their Adamesque satin wood cabinet at the Paris Exhibition of 1867. By November 1868 the *Building News* reported "... some of our best artists and designers have left their medieval love

Plate 41. The 'Bulwer', sold by Hamptons early in the twentieth century, price £8 8s. It is a near reproduction of what was mistakenly thought to be a Cromwellian type of chair.

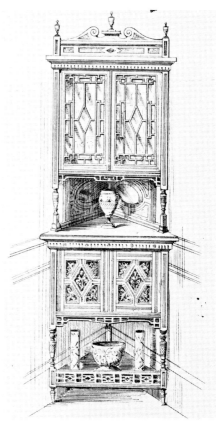

Plate 42. Rosewood drawing room suite and corner cabinet by Shoolbreds, selected for publicity in Cabinet Maker *in August 1880 because it represented "the prevailing style of the day, a free treatment of Queen Anne." Certainly not derived from genuine Queen Anne furniture or architecture, the term here implies merely the application of a few eighteenth century details.*

Plate 45. High quality Chippendale inspired cabinet stamped Edwards and Roberts, late nineteenth century.
Courtesy Victoria and Albert Museum.

and gone clean over to the camp of those who extol the relics of the days of Queen Anne" which, as Mrs. Haweis explained, implied the whole eighteenth century.

These styles gained much patriotic support because they were English.

QUEEN ANNE

'Queen Anne' was the most used name but it certainly did not refer to the cabriole legs, curved splat back chairs, fine marquetry and burr veneers of genuine Queen Anne furniture. This is not surprising, as the *Cabinet Maker* lamented in June 1881: "... there is a deplorable absence of illustrated literature having to do with early eighteenth century house furnishing" So, 'Curator' suggested in 1882,[12] "I should advise the designer to study the lines of the architects rather than those of the furniture makers."

So it was that some Victorian 'Queen Anne' furniture had heavy cornices and pediments, curved gable ends, dentil ornamentation and urns to echo the Queen Anne revival in architecture. Some examples appear in Plates 42 and 43. That drawing room suite was considered in 1880 "to represent the prevailing style of the day a free treatment of Queen Anne". Some of the more subtle furniture in this manner is discussed in Chapter 4.

Unfortunately, the name was applied indiscriminately, even to such horrors as the tea tables covered in stamped silk plush with fancy fringes in Plate 44, as well as to many only vaguely eighteenth century-ish pieces.

Whilst not strictly furniture, it is worth remembering that the Queen Anne architectural revival introduced several 'novel features' which affected furnishing schemes. These were windows with small panes on either side of a central arch, doors with light pediments or arrangements on top for the display of china, window seats and wooden mantels.

CHIPPENDALE

This became immensely popular for dining rooms, the splendid chairs offering prestige and comfort. The name implied many things from Edwards and Roberts' quality pieces (Plate 45) to the 'new and modified Chippendale' by Messrs North of High Wycombe which "will be welcome in rooms where the somewhat clumsy originals would have to be excluded." Sometimes the name merely implied 'mahogany' and

Plate 43. Dressing table in 'Victorian Queen Anne', 1886, "... the little pediments on top of the glass, the shaped pieces at the sides and the quaint details in the doors are appropriate in feeling to the Victorian Queen Anne sort of architecture which is now so much in vogue". Cabinet Maker, July 1886.

Plate 44. Description 'Queen Anne' totally irrelevantly applied even to these impracticable tables covered with stamped silk plush. Made by Jacobs and Co. Leicester, 1880.

Plate 46. *Near Chippendale style settee and chair, c.1900.*

Gillows do not seem to have been aware of the contradiction in their caption: "A Chippendale bookcase and other furniture specially designed for and manufactured by Gillows." Plate 47 shows a well stretched example of revived Chippendalia.

Plate 47. Impressive example of revived Chippendalia, c.1900.

48

A DRAWING-ROOM IN THE ADAMS' STYLE.

Plate 48. 'Adams' drawing room in early twentieth century catalogue of Hamptons, showing lack of understanding of Adam's work. Below, bed-chamber in the 'Adams' style in Shoolbred's 1889 catalogue.

BED-CHAMBER IN THE "ADAMS" STYLE   JAMES SHOOLBRED & COMPY
TOTTENHAM HOUSE, TOTTENHAM COURT ROAD, W.

ADAM

The 'Adams' style, as it was called, was a popular prestigious style throughout this period. Gillows showed the Adam interiors which they had exhibited at the Paris Exhibition of 1878 again in the Fine Art and Industries Exhibition in Manchester in 1882. Bradley Thomas Batsford helpfully published a reprint of *The Architecture, Decoration and Furniture of R & J Adam,* costing £1 5s. in 1881. "How admirably the Adams' style lends itself to the chaste decoration of bedroom furniture" commended the *Cabinet Maker* in April 1881, illustrating a dressing table with shield shaped mirror and 'Adams' bedroom suite featured in most catalogues as in Plate 48. The mode lent itself to the vogue for white painted bedroom furniture in the 80s and 90s and was popular for drawing rooms. Plate 48. Many items were, of course, copied from the domesticised 'Adam' of Hepplewhite but, strangely, his name does not seem to have had the sales appeal of the other eighteenth century designers.

Kate Warren Clouston who, in 1897, wrote *The Chippendale Period in English Furniture,* at the request of Debenham and Freebody, presumably to encourage sales of their new and antique furniture, gave Adam high praise.

Plate 49. Triple shield back satin wood settee with cane seat and well painted with floral swags, c.1900, in manner of 1790s.

SHERATON

The *Magazine of Art*[13] noted in 1883: "In recent years a fashion for Sheraton's furniture has sprung up and has so widely spread that modern cabinet makers have found it worth their while to reproduce many specimens and even to attempt original work in the same style." It was specially popular for bedrooms (Plates 50 to 52) and drawing rooms.

There was a complete reprint of Sheraton's *Drawing Book* in 1895, price 50s. Unfortunately the slenderness of some Sheraton forms tempted some economising makers to slim them further and there is often a meanness about the results.

Plate 50. Rather heavy, enamelled interpretation of Sheraton toilet table in Plate 51.

Plate 52. Late eighteenth century details applied to bedroom suite, c.1900.

Plate 51. A Hindley and Wilkinson exact reproduction of the Sheraton toilet table in the Victoria and Albert Museum, c.1900.

MOORISH FURNITURE.
made in Cairo.
Imported by
MESSRS ROTTMANN, STROME & CO.

Plate 53, left. Moorish furniture, made in Cairo and imported by Rottmann, Strome and Co. Cabinet Maker, February 1886.

Plate 54. Koran stand (centre) and other Moorish furniture, 1880s.

Plate 56. 'Arab' table bought for Standen, labelled and impressed 'Liberty and Co., 263 Regent Street, London,' c.1890.

MOORISH MORESQUE

Who first popularised the Moresque and when is not clear. A 'Moorish Piano Case' exhibited at the 1872 International Exhibition had provoked the *Builders News* to comment that it was "fairly designed in the style chosen, but why the choice? Is it going to Morocco?" Libertys which had opened as an oriental warehouse in 1875 certainly sold 'Arabian' sideboards, wardrobes and writing tables and Koran stands as in Plates 53 and 54, imported from Cairo in the 80s, but the *Cabinet Maker's* remark in May, 1884, that "Anglo-Moresque and other fancies have had a good innings" suggests that perhaps the fashion started in the late 70s. One of its leaders was the firm of H. & J. Cooper.

It was not only individual Cairene items decorated with panels of Musharabyeh turning that were popular but also whole decorative schemes. It was not only Libertys who offered Moorish/Saracenic Smoking rooms; even Gillows decorated the entrance hall of the Royal Pavilion at the International Health Exhibition in 1884 in the Moorish manner with much Musharabyeh panelling and brilliant colours.

Plate 55 shows three Anglo-Moresque chairs by Liberty in 1884. Not all the detail is strictly Moorish and, of course, the style was applied to

Plate 55. Anglo-Moresque chairs by Liberty, Cabinet Maker, April 1884.

Plate 57. Anglo-Japanese writing table and chairs from Furniture Trade Catalogue, *1882.*

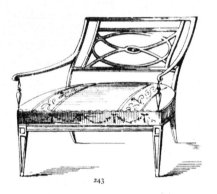

distinctly non-Moorish items as when in 1883 an article gave instructions on *How to make a Moresque Hat Stand.* H. & J. Cooper were said to be "still leaders in the Cairene department" in 1885 and Libertys offered much of it into the 90s. The little 'Arab' table in Plate 56 is impressed and labelled 'Liberty & Co' and is probably an example of their own production in this genre. In 1886 there was a 'Studio of Arabian and Persian Art' in Notting Hill Gate staffed by "Asiatic Artists under the supervision of the late Chief Designer for the Decoration and Furnishing of Palaces ... to the late Sultan Abd-ul-Aziz",[14] so presumably there was a considerable Moorish taste to be catered for. Certainly J.S. Henry, one of the most advanced suppliers, was still offering Moorish in 1887.[15]

ANGLO-JAPANESE

Japanese artefacts were seen by many for the first time when the varied collection of the first British consul to Japan, Sir Rutherford Alcock, was on view at the International Exhibition of 1862. There was little furniture as Japanese houses were minimally furnished with small cabinets, kimono stands and low tables, their occupants sitting and sleeping on Tatami mats on the floor. But such was the enthusiasm of fashionable aesthetic taste in the 1870s and 80s for Japanese prints, ceramics, fans, clothes, etc. that furniture with a Japanese flavour was needed to accompany them.

Some astoundingly original furniture (Plate 70) which will be discussed in Chapter 4, was designed in the 1860s and 70s by the architect Edward Godwin, who solved non-Japanese but western needs for sideboards and bedroom suites through Japanese insights. Some of his taut, controlled designs — his coffee table and the asymmetrical fretwork brackets which appeared in the *Cabinet Maker's Pattern Book* of 1877 were plagiarized by the trade, but the ideas behind his designs were little understood and 'Anglo-Japanese' came often to mean over elaborately fretted work, as in Plate 58: "Bedchamber furniture in the Japanese style" advertised by Shoolbreds for about a decade from 1874. Plate 59 shows a more restrained suite in ash and ebonized woods at Whiteleys in 1881. Plate 60, a display cabinet in the

JAMES SHOOLBRED & COMP.Y TOTTENHAM HOUSE, TOTTENHAM COURT ROAD, W.

Japanese taste, bears the label of George Maddox of 21 Baker Street and was probably made in the 1870s. Many examples were inset with panels of carved boxwood or embossed leather.

How far the popularity of Japanese forms lasted into the 1880s is not clear but the obituary of Godwin[16] in 1886 refers to the Anglo-Japanese style "which was in vogue some few years since" and certainly the early 1890s' Shoolbred catalogue no longer showed the Anglo-Japanese bedroom which had been in their other catalogues since 1874; so presumably the taste waned in the 80s.

With Anglo-Japanese having lost favour in the 80s and Moorish in the 90s and French work being produced mainly only at the most expensive levels, it was English styles which held the field at the beginning of the twentieth century. This is hardly surprising in that era of intense nationalism, Kipling and the Pomp and Circumstance marches. The editor of the *Cabinet Maker,* considering the state of affairs after the Queen's Diamond Jubilee in 1897, thought "No phase of our *fin de siècle* furniture has been more pleasing than the 'run' on the style of Chippendale and his immediate successors. When its history comes to be written the revival of the Georgian modes will undoubtedly

Plate 58. Bedroom furniture in Japanese style illustrated in Shoolbred's catalogue from 1874 to at least 1882.

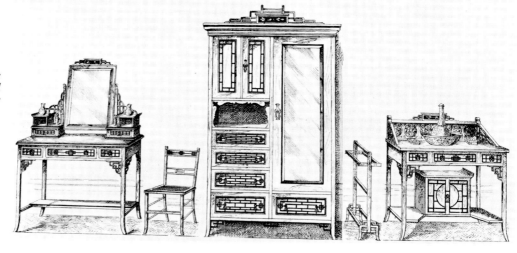

Plate 59. Anglo-Japanese bedroom suite in ash and ebonized woods sold by William Whiteley, 1881. Cabinet Maker.

Plate 60. Display cabinet labelled 'George Maddox, Upholsterer, 21 Baker Street, Manufactory 21 Blandford Mews.' He was in Baker Street 1860-85 but seems to have left Blandford Mews in 1871 or '72. But he may have continued to use old labels so this may be of the 1870s or 80s. An upper central section has been removed.

rank as the distinctest and perhaps the most important epoch of the century."

Well hardly, but repro does seem to be an all too persistent British addiction. Even the early Victorian forms which were still in vogue in the 1880s came in for a revival at the end of this third of a century according to the catalogue of Jas. Shoolbred and Co., c.1910. "In the Specimen Rooms . . . From the masterpieces of Adam, Chippendale, Sheraton and the English Renaissance generally one passes to the practical solidity of early Victorian lines, now once again attaining a certain vogue." Whilst The Award at the 1977 Furniture Exhibition at Earls Court went to Mackintoshs of Kirkcaldy for near reproductions of pieces designed by Charles Rennie Mackintosh around 1900.

Almost all the major British exhibits at the St. Louis Exhibition in 1904 were repro Georgian; and it so continued to dominate production that *The Studio Year Book* of 1911 reported: "In surveying the work which has been produced during the last few years one cannot fail to be impressed by the prevailing lack of originality in design. The few attempts made to break away from accepted models have in most cases ended in failure, while in nearly all directions we find nothing but reproductions of the old styles."

Footnotes

1. *Artist and Journal of Home Culture*, Vol. 1, p.244, August 1880, quotes from an editorial in *Furniture Gazette*. Christopher Dresser editor of the latter throughout 1880.
2. *Original Sketches for Art Furniture 1877-79*. Not all copies have text; the Bodleian's has.
3. *Artist and Journal of Home Culture*, Vol. 3, p.55, February 1, 1882, quotes review in *Cabinet Maker*.
4. J.H. Bardwell. *Two Centuries of Soho, by the clergy of St Anne's*, 1898. pp.185-6.
5. Hindley and Wilkinson Ltd. catalogue, 1900-12, caption to Plate XII.
6. *Building News*, Vol. 41, p.319, September 9, 1881.
7. *Cabinet Maker*, Vol. 12, pp.57-62, September 1891.
8. Illustrated Catalogue of Paris International Exhibition 1878, pp.200-1, and elsewhere.
9. Hindley and Wilkinson Ltd. catalogue, 1900-12, caption to Plate VII.
10. See H. Binstead, *English Chairs*, pub. John Tiranti, 1923, pl. X.
11. *Cabinet Maker*, Vol. 7, p.231, July 1, 1886.
12. *Cabinet Maker*, Vol. 2, p.175, March 1, 1882.
13. *Magazine of Art*, Eustace Balfour: Sheraton's Furniture, 1883, p.190-6.
14. Advertisement, p.2, Kelly's Directory of Cabinet, Furniture and Upholstery Trades, 2nd edition, 1886.
15. *Cabinet Maker*, Vol. 7, p.277, April 1, 1887.
16. *Cabinet Maker*, Vol. 7, p.147.

CHAPTER 4

Original Designs and Art Furniture

Chapter 3 sketched the popularity throughout the whole period 1880-1915 of furniture made more and less in the styles of other times and other lands. This chapter explores the more original work being produced then and investigates what was and what should be understood by the term 'art furniture'.

Having seen the furniture trade so preoccupied with reproduction work, it is rather startling to find the *Cabinet Maker* of January 1882 discussing " the modern furniture revolution" and the designer J. Moyr Smith, reminiscing in 1887[1] about "the new style of decoration and furniture taking hold of the public" in the 70s. To find out about this new style, which was modern in the 1870s and 80s, it is necessary to step back to the 60s and even earlier.

Plate 61. Massive oak cabinet in a new bold form of gothic designed by the architect J.P. Seddon and exhibited in 1862. Panels painted by Madox Brown, Burne-Jones, Rossetti and Morris.
Courtesy Victoria and Albert Museum.

Plate 62. Three designs by Charles Lock Eastlake and a recommended splayed leg table, all from Hints on Household Taste, 1868. Note the plank legs of the wash-stand, the brought forward plank sides of the chest of drawers and the 'revealed' construction.

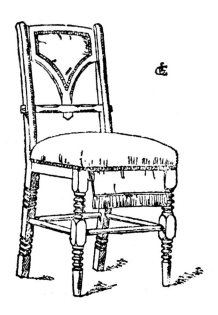

Philosophies of design had been debated for decades. Pugin, the Pre-Raphaelites, Ruskin and Morris, among others, had called for simplicity and honesty in art generally in the 1840s and 50s. Pugin had created inspired new forms for the House of Lords; and concern at the elaborate tastelessness of many exhibits at the Great Exhibition had caused other architects to turn to designing furniture. William Butterfield, for example, designed some very rectilinear pieces in the mid 50s, whilst J.P. Seddon's massive, much chamfered, four square cabinet (Plate 61), and Norman Shaw's gothic bookcase (Plate 12), were seen at the 1862 Exhibition in London. When William Morris set up house in 1856 and the architect Edward William Godwin in 1867 both found the furniture then available in the shops unacceptable and proceeded to design their own. All these and others prepared the way, inaugurating, as Mrs. Haweis put it, "a kind of Reformed Faith in art".

But in the late 1860s and early 70s several publications spread the design debate to a wider public in homes and workshops. Charles Lock Eastlake's *Hints on Household Taste*, 1868,[2] was a powerful book capable of winning over its readers to want honest construction, rational forms and minimal but appropriate decoration. Plate 62. He had an exhilarating DIY approach: "Seek out" he urged "an intelligent carpenter (one who does not work for the trade will be best)" who "ought by the aid of a few hints and sketches to turn out a more workmanlike and picturesque object . . . Order what article you require to be made in solid wood (mahogany) and either simply rubbed with boiled oil or if they must be stained at all let them be stained black".

Plate 63a, a very heavy chair with simple carving and the rarely seen deeply v-cut lines, may be by an amateur designer following Eastlake's advice, whilst Plate 63b shows a professional interpretation.

Plate 63a. Very heavy low chair presumably by amateur designer following Eastlake's DIY approach.

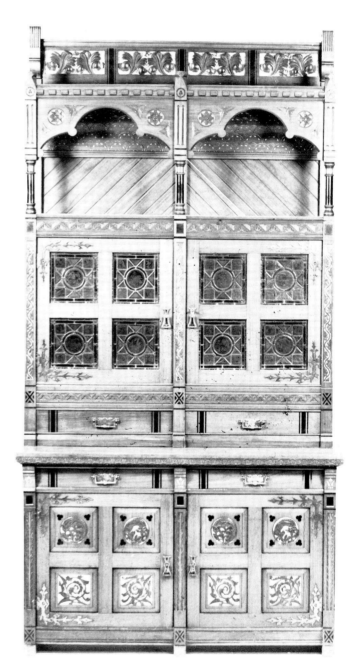

Plate 63b. Oak and gilt cabinet which partly resembles a design in the second edition of Hints, *1870s.*

Plate 64. Elaborate revivalist gothic designs from Bruce Talbert's Gothic Forms Applied to Furniture, *1867.*

THE INFLUENCE OF BRUCE TALBERT

Eastlake's book must have helped to create a favourable climate for the recently published *Gothic Forms Applied to Furniture* by Bruce Talbert, the young designer from Dundee. This contained some elaborate revivalist gothic as in Plate 64, but also simpler, less ecclesiastical and more domesticised designs like Plate 65, which were in tune with Eastlake's demands. Equally sober rather secular gothic by Seddon (Plate 61) had been seen at the 1862 Exhibition and looking now at Talbert's designs it is difficult to detect anything very revolutionary, but, according to Moyr Smith in *Ornamental Interiors*, 1887, "plates from *Gothic Forms* were undoubtedly the cause of the new style of decoration and furniture taking hold of the public for the book soon found its way to the chief designers and cabinet makers in the kingdom". Perhaps its impact was due to the fact that very few new books of designs had been published for a long time; and perhaps the many people repelled by the ritualist, high church associations of previous gothic furniture, were won over by Talbert's more secular, homely decorations including carvings of birds and animals.

His early "true and orthodox rabbit hutch" style was followed by lighter and simpler designs as in Plate 66. Plate 67 shows a drawing room cabinet he designed to be finished in dull black and a little gilt.

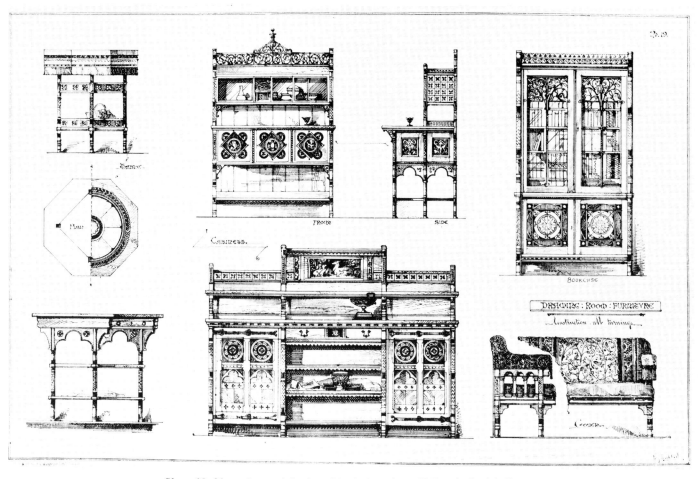

Plate 65. More domesticised gothic designs from Talbert's Gothic Forms.

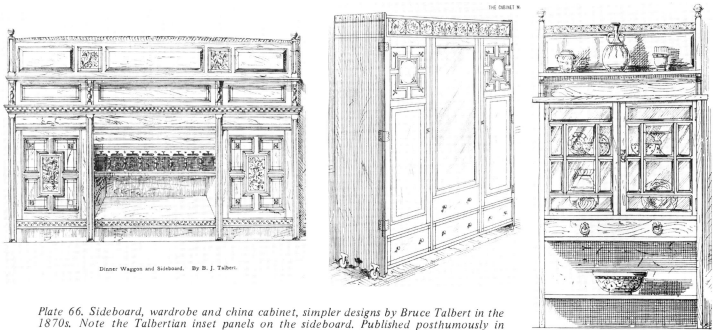

Dinner Waggon and Sideboard. By B. J. Talbert.

Plate 66. Sideboard, wardrobe and china cabinet, simpler designs by Bruce Talbert in the 1870s. Note the Talbertian inset panels on the sideboard. Published posthumously in Cabinet Maker.

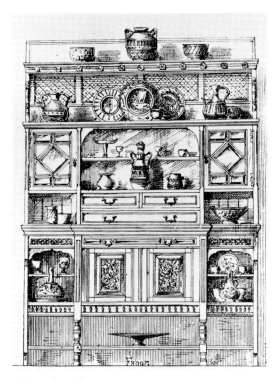

Plate 67. *Drawing room cabinet designed by Bruce Talbert to be finished in dull black and a little gilt, early 1870s. Published posthumously in* Cabinet Maker.

Looking back in 1882, soon after Talbert's early death, the *Cabinet Maker* judged this "one of the very first of this type" which "marks the reform the designer brought about in such matters over the old chiffonier". Plate 68 shows his famous 'Pet' sideboard of 1873 made by Gillows. They must have been impressed by his simpler designs because two of their only four exhibits at the 1872 International Exhibition were his angle *étagère*, priced £10 15s., and his ebonized cabinet at £27 10s. He had by then set up his own design practice and supplied many firms including Hollands, Jackson and Graham, and Marsh, Jones and Cribb.

What then were the characteristics — though they were not all innovations — of the Talbertian or 'progressive' revolution of the 1870s?

— straight lines, long strap hinges and ring handles
— the enrichment of mouldings with dentils and other architecturally inspired ornaments
— tongue and groove planking sometimes set diagonally
— cut through work and rows of spindles
— applied enamelled plaques and painted panels
— inlay and occasional appropriate low relief carving in place of 'unmeaning scrolls'
— revealed construction showing dovetails and tenons
— the inset panel
— unstained oak merely oiled

The spindles popularised by Talbert were readily and cheaply available from turners working at rented powered lathes in the big saw

Plate 68. *Bruce Talbert's 'Pet' sideboard made by Gillows, 1873, in oak with carved creatures, foliage and quotation.* Courtesy Victoria and Albert Museum.

mills in the East End. Unfortunately, Talbert gave in his 1876 book[3] a Flemish recipe "tried with success in Dundee" for fuming oak and so must have encouraged the spread of the often unattractive colouring which it produced.

WALFORD AND DONKIN

Talbert's obituary saluted him as "the pioneer of simplicity in modern furniture" and "the creator of an epoch"[4] but, of course, there were other reformer designers and, as usual, it is difficult to assess who influenced whom. In 1868 the much read *Building News* featured furniture (Plate 69) by the architects Walford and Donkin, not because the shapes, except those of chairs, were remarkable but because these designers had for some time been advocating "ebonized furniture decorated with fret cutting, stencilling, incising and turning" which processes "have not been extensively used in the same manner and consequently we have to thank these gentlemen for pointing out to us the tools we have at our command".[5] It is significant that these processes were to provide the characteristic ingredients in the coming style.

Plate 69. Art Furniture designed by the architects Walford and Donkin in or before 1868. They were early advocates of ebonizing, fret cutting and incised decoration. The incised lines of the horses and chariots on the front of the sideboard were in gilt on the black. Note the legs and sides of the chair are formed from single planks. Building News, *December 24, 1868.*

Ebonizing had already been taken up by E.W. Godwin whose Anglo-Japanese furniture was mentioned briefly in the previous chapter, but here it is necessary to consider his importance as a creative, original designer. He had designed gothic town halls and Jacobean furniture and thought old forms should be carefully studied, but his famous cabinet of 1867 (Plate 70), is an astonishingly original achievement. Here is a western need solved not by copying Japanese forms — they did not have or need sideboard/cabinets — but with Japanese insights: the pared down puritan approach, the less-is-more gospel with its creative use of voids and plain surfaces. Other examples of Godwin's approach are the coffee table, wine cabinet, sideboard, sofa and bedroom furniture in Plates 71 and 72. Some of his designs, notably the coffee table, were plagiarised by the trade in the 70s so although the bulk of his work was not generally available until William Watt, who manufactured it, brought out his catalogue *Art Furniture* in 1877, Godwin must already have had some influence for most of a decade. The catalogue was in such demand that it was reissued the following year so, presumably, a good deal of this startling furniture sold. Little has yet been found. Where is it?

Plate 70. Ebonized sideboard designed c.1867 by Edward Godwin and made by William Watt. Inspired by Japanese concepts, this is one of the many original designs by Godwin published in Watt's catalogue Art Furniture, 1877.
Courtesy Sotheby's Belgravia.

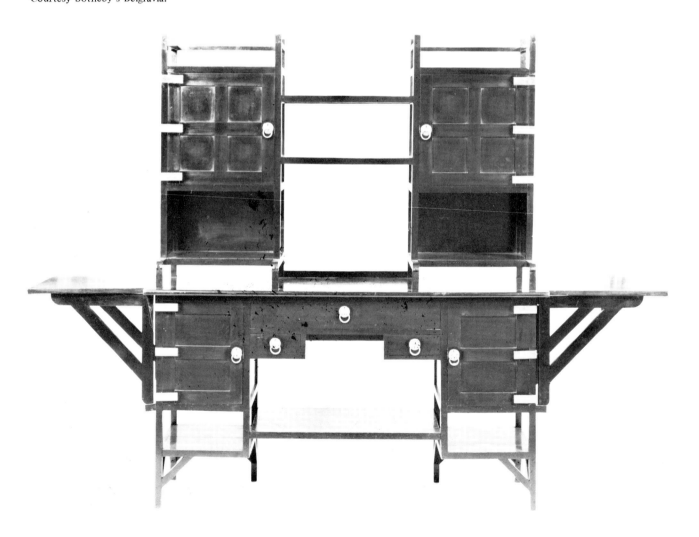

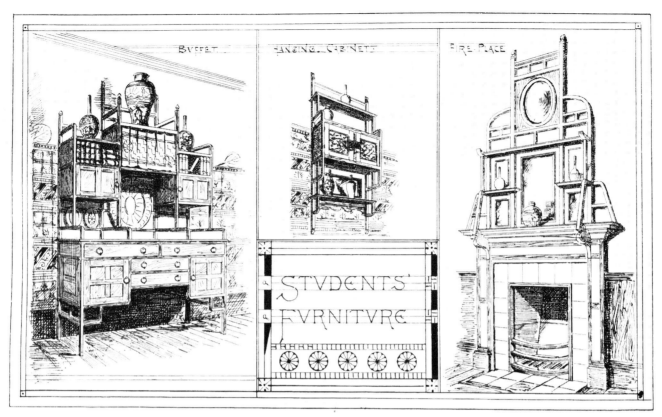

Plate 71. Plates from William Watt's catalogue Art Furniture, *1877, designed earlier by Edward Godwin.*

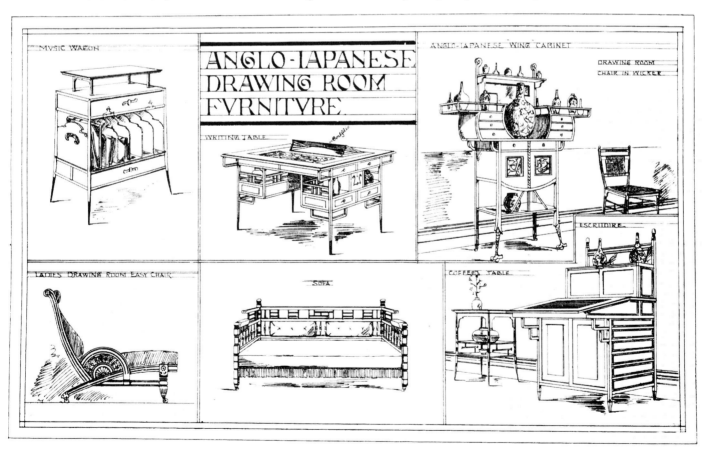

BED ROOM FVRNITVRE

LARGE PAINTED WARDROBE

ANGLO-JAPANESE WARDROBE

ANGLO-TABLE JAPANESE DRESSING-

ANGLO-JAPANESE WASH STAND

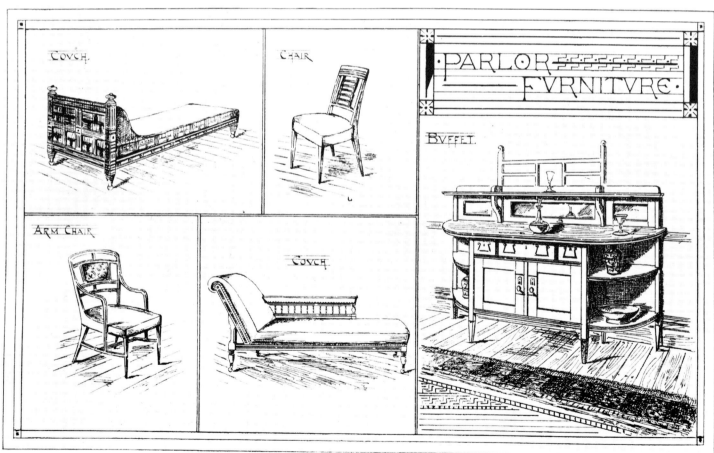

COVCH.

CHAIR

ARM CHAIR

COVCH

PARLOR FVRNITVRE

BVFFET.

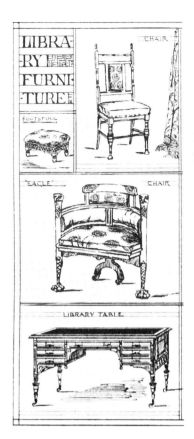

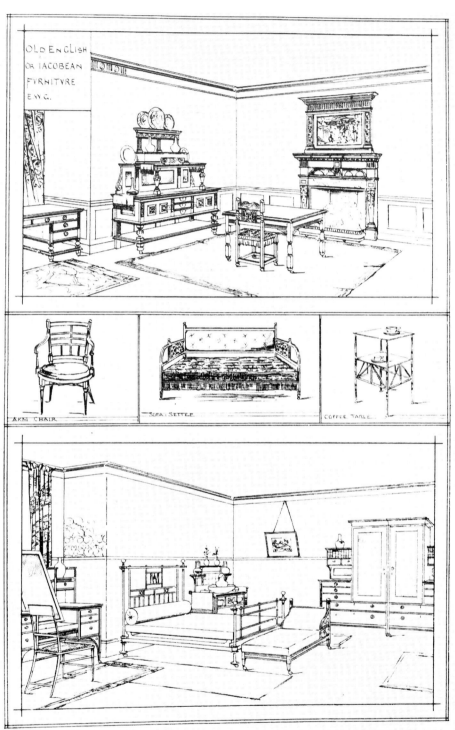

Plate 72. More plates from Watts's catalogue showing designs by Godwin. Note influential tall pinnacles on wardrobe and innovation of attached towel rails.

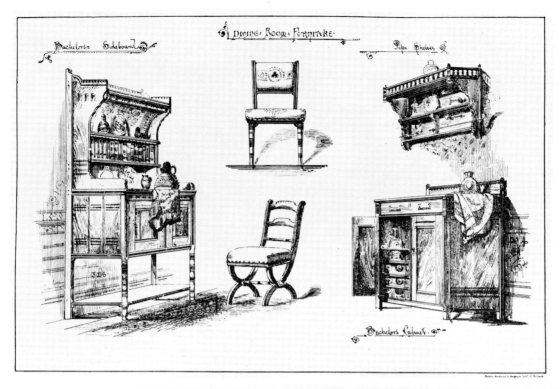

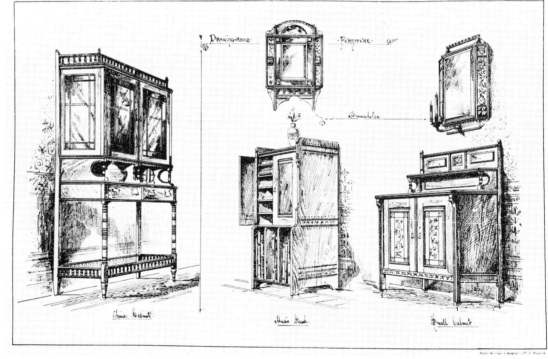

Plate 73. From Collinson and Lock's influential catalogue Sketches of Artistic Furniture, *1871. Note the spindles and how the plank sides of the music stand are brought forward as recommended by Eastlake.*

THE INFLUENCE OF COLLINSON AND LOCK'S CATALOGUE

Moyr Smith tells of another influential publication: "Shortly after the appearance of Talbert's book the firm of Collinson and Lock, which was about the first to recognize the vitality of new style, brought out their catalogue. The subjects were treated in a much plainer, simpler and lighter manner than those by Talbert and in some cases were as bare of ornament as it was possible to be; but there was practical knowledge displayed in the selection and the work was simple enough to be easily wrought, so that the examples given in the catalogue were imitated all over the country and helped greatly to influence the new style."[6]

Plates 73 and 74 show some of the simplest pieces in the Collinson and Lock catalogue *Sketches of Artistic Furniture,* 1871. The sturdy construction and the brought forward sides of the music cabinet were features commended by Eastlake, whilst the plank ends of the chest of drawers anticipated 'progressive' end of the century furniture. Curiously, Moyr Smith does not mention who was responsible for the *Sketches* except to say that he 'contributed some designs'. It is usually assumed that the architect T.E. Collcutt produced most of them but perhaps they were the work of an as yet unrecognised trade designer.

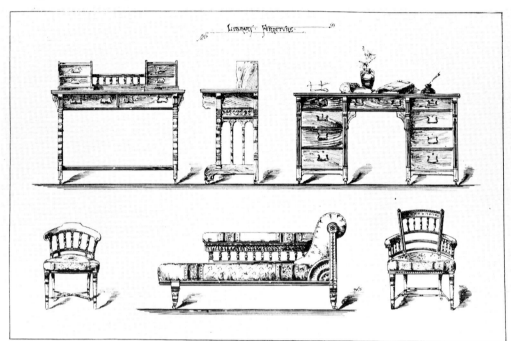

Plate 74. More from the Collinson and Lock catalogue of 1871.

THE INFLUENCE OF T.E. COLLCUTT

But, certainly, it was Collcutt who took the furniture revolution notably and acceptably further with his influential ebonized cabinet (Plate 75) which Collinson and Lock made for the International Exhibition of 1871. This interesting piece with its open ended, more lightweight and highly finished appearance must have seemed very desirably and excitingly new. J.H. Pollen in his official report on the Exhibition enthused: "It is full of ingenious little drawers, shelves and receptacles reminding us in this respect of the quaint devices of Japanese cabinet makers. The central portion of the upper and lower stages is shut in by doors. These are panelled and the panels occupied by classical figures painted in white on vermilion and with birds all admirably drawn. The dark wood (mahogany stained black) is covered with arabesque painted ornament and the supports at the angles turned on the lathe. They have delicate strings and neckings but no violent lumps or protuberances."

Such refined features are seen in the best of the "modern black and gold furniture" which came to be produced in the 70s and 80s — Plates 76 to 80 show good examples. The characteristics of this furniture may be summarised as: straight lines, spindles, brackets and many shelves

Plate 76. Art aesthetic movement ebonized and painted side cabinet. The painted panels are inscribed Morning, Music, Chess, Night, Billiards and Whist, c.1880. 98in. x 69in.
Courtesy Sotheby's Belgravia.

often backed with bevelled glass, incised lines, rings and linear patterns, painted and stencilled panels and some low relief carving especially of sunflowers and lunettes. It was often finished in dull black or ebonized and gilded but also produced in oiled or fumed natural woods and sometimes painted. Plates 81-83.

It was then Talbert, Walford and Donkin, Godwin, Collcutt and others who, before 1880, had produced alternatives to the heavy and curvaceous Victorian and the popular repro styles. The simpler, restrained furniture of Talbert and the Collinson and Lock catalogue are early examples of the 'progressive' furniture of the end of the century; but what should the other be-spindled, bracketed, mainly ebonized be

Plate 77. Ebonized octagonal breakfast table, the gilded frieze painted with ivy leaves. Gilt incised rings on legs. An attractive example of art furniture.
Courtesy Sotheby's Belgravia.

71

Plate 78. Art aesthetic movement ebonized beechwood and painted side cabinet. Cupboard doors painted with birds, c.1880, 75½in. x 72in.
Courtesy Sotheby's Belgravia.

Plate 80. Ebonized armchair designed by E.W. Godwin.
Courtesy Sotheby's Belgravia.

called? It has become customary now to refer to it as 'art furniture' even though during its heyday that term had a variety of other meanings. Collinson and Lock, for example, advertised progressive Talbertian designs as "Art Furniture in the old English style" and the designer, A. Jonquet, entitled his book *Original Sketches for Art Furniture in the Jacobean, Queen Anne, Adam and other Styles*, 1877-79, whilst the *Cabinet Maker* noted in February 1885 that "modern furnishing is now indiscriminately called — art furnishing."

But because the be-spindled and mainly ebonized was the new, original furniture of the 1870s and 80s, and because they were notable as the decades of the art aesthetic movement it seems reasonable now to limit the meaning of 'art furniture' to that type. It should be studied in the context of the various theories of decoration that were debated in those decades of the aesthetic movement.

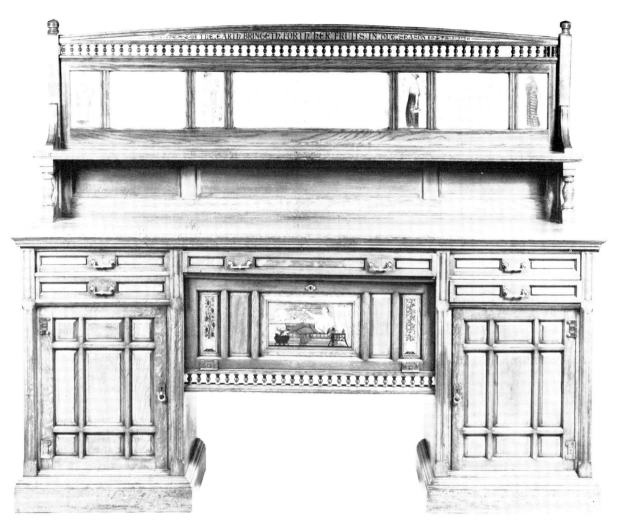

Plate 79. An unstained example of art furniture, an oak sideboard with inscription 'The Earth Bringeth Forth Her Fruits in Due Season', mirrors in superstructure and painted panels of Spring, Summer, Autumn and Winter. The central cupboard has a fall front painted with a reclining maiden, 1870s. 69in. x 84in.
Courtesy Sotheby's Belgravia.

THE AESTHETIC MOVEMENT

Blown by breezes from many exhibitions and the contradictory currents of Ruskin, a tide of aestheticism had flooded into middle class circles in the 1870s and 80s. It had become trendy and exciting to discuss art matters and to take art magazines — the *Magazine of Art*, 1878, *The Artist and Journal of Home Culture*, 1880 — and to read the *Art in the Home* series[7] aimed at "the cultivated middle class, able to enjoy leisure, refinement and luxury in moderation". It was the time to debate decoration, to display 'art pottery' and wear 'art clothes'.

The more intellectual read of art giving "the highest quality to your moments" in Walter Pater's *Studies in the History of the Renaissance*, 1873. Max Beerbohm wrote in 1880 of aesthetes "hurling their mahogany into the streets". Pillars, like Gladstone and Dickens, collected ceramics not only aesthetes like Oscar Wilde and Whistler; and Mr. 'Philistine' Jones had begun to think about the shape of his jugs.[8]

The art seeker need no longer fear condemnation as an 'aesthetic crotchet'; it was not only trendy and exciting, it was even respectable to be concerned about 'art' matters despite *Punch's* mockery, and Gilbert and Sullivan's parody of aestheticism in *Patience*, 1881.

It was thus inevitable that the alert furniture trade, keen to catch the tide, should foster the concept of 'art furniture'. An Art Furniture Company associated with Godwin existed briefly in 1867-68, but a Julius Jacoby was the first to be entered in the category of 'Artistic Furniture Manufacturers' when it first appeared in the London Post Office Directory in 1869. By the mid 70s a dozen makers were listed, including some old established firms previously content to appear as cabinet makers. Art had become a word to conjure with, the key word in advertising and sales talk and so it was used very indiscriminately.

Indiscriminate too, came to be the application of the ingredients of the art furniture of our limited definition. Many pieces were so fussily encumbered with brackets, shelves, spindles and balusters that it came to be known as the 'bracket and overmantel style'. It was cheap to produce and a good deal of it is of shoddy quality. It has never been popular with dealers, possibly because so much dull black has become depressingly dingy — though surely this is revivable when a piece merits it? In the many decades when it has not been marketable, much may have been broken up so it is difficult to estimate how much is available.

Plate 84. Hall cupboard designed by Rhoda and Agnes Garrett for James and Margaret Beale's Holland Park house in 1875, a subtly proportioned, architectural piece in what the Garretts referred to as the 'Queen Anne' style.
Courtesy Dr. Jonathan Wager.

Plate 85. A Collinson and Lock rosewood cabinet shown at the 1878 Paris Exhibition. It has the broken pediment, dentils and pilasters characteristic of Queen Anne architecture.

VICTORIAN ARCHITECTURAL 'QUEEN ANNE'

Alongside that often black art furniture, the simple, plainish pieces and repro, there was in the 1870s and 80s other rather subtle furniture which does not fit into these categories. Plate 84 shows an important example, a hall cabinet designed in 1875 by the forceful furnishers Rhoda and Agnes Garrett. They would have referred to this as in the Queen Anne style because, whilst urging that "simplicity of form and delicacy of detail are the fundamental rules", they sought their inspiration mainly in classical architecture as reinterpreted early in the eighteenth century. The incised balusters contrast rather oddly with the pillars and pilasters above but this is a subtly proportioned piece. Plate 85 shows a Collinson and Lock design in this manner. Plate 86 of designs from the *Cabinet Makers Pattern Book* (3rd and 5th series, 1882 and n.d., but mid-80s) shows that this Victorian Queen Anne with architectural cornices, broken pediments, dentils, urns and columns, etc., was by then a feature of general trade. This may well have been the outcome of the advice given by 'Curator' in 1882:[9] "In designing modern Queen Anne I should advise the designer to study the lines of the architects rather than those of the furniture makers; not by any means making his furniture architectural in character but picking from

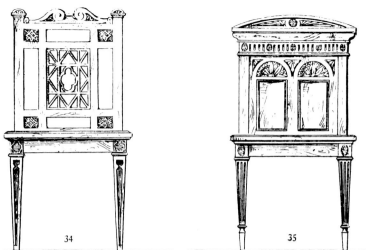

34   35

Plate 86. Sketches from Cabinet Makers Pattern Book, *third series 1882, fifth n.d. Chairs top left from third, other items from fifth series. All show that early eighteenth century architectural features decorated stock furniture in the mid-1880s.*

old sources his mouldings, enrichments and carvings. . . In this way furniture may be designed and legitimately called Queen Anne without having any resemblance to the article actually made from 1702-14.''

The name 'Victorian Queen Anne' is not very satisfactory because it implies reproductions, whereas these pieces stem from an attempt to create a new style. Perhaps what they are called, 'architectural Anne' or 'freed Renaissance' or whatever, does not matter so much but it is necessary to recognize that this other trend towards simplicity but incorporating the elements of Queen Anne architecture did exist from the 1870s and should be recognised as a new style. Plates 87 and 88 show items by the architects John Small and Maurice B. Adams who were designing in this manner.

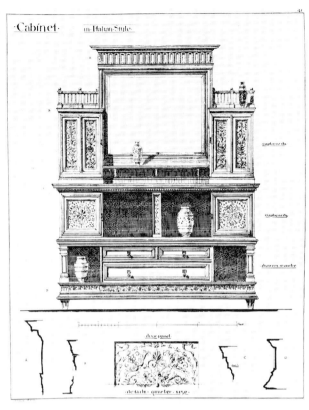

Plate 87. The Scottish architect John Small designed this cabinet in the Italian (i.e. Renaissance) style "which", he wrote in 1883, "Authorities are telling us is the coming style. All the details of this cabinet have been culled from the purest old examples of that period."

Plate 88. Bedroom suite in hard woods designed by Maurice B. Adams, FRIBA, and made by Gillow and Co. in a dignified, partly architectural manner. From Adams' Examples of Old English Houses and Furniture with some modern works from designs by the author, *1888.*

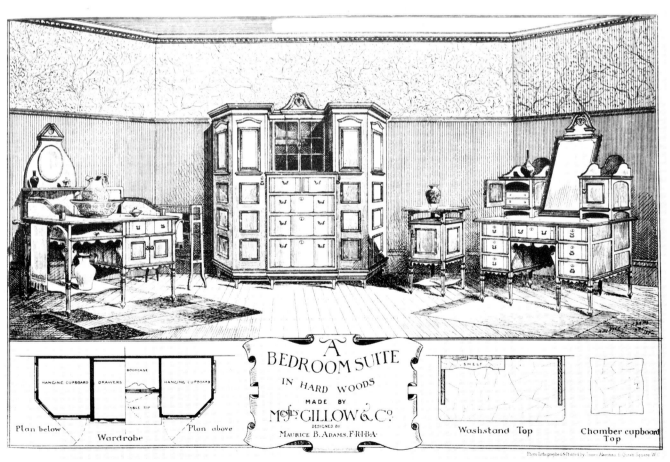

Plate 89. Jackson and Graham's cabinet illustrated by Robert Edis in Furniture and Decoration of Town Houses, 1881. In mahogany or American walnut with the cupboard doors 'formed with Chinese paintings on panels', estimated cost £16.

SIMPLER DESIGN RELATED TO MECHANISATION

The movement towards simpler and more rational furnishing received a boost from the well publicised Cantor Lectures of 1880 given by the architect Col. Robert Edis and published as the *Furniture and Decoration of Town Houses,* 1881. In it he praised Morris & Co., Grace, Gillow, Jackson & Graham, Holland & Sons and Trollope & Co. "the best of our cabinet makers" for "having for the most part shown a desire to substitute general simplicity of form and detail for extravagance and eccentricity of design and construction". He wrote of Plate 89, the Jackson & Graham cabinet, that it "... seems to me to combine general artistic merit of design with simplicity and practical common sense in form and arrangement; it adapts itself equally well for books and china with well arranged cupboard space for books and ladies' work; the fronts of these cupboards are formed with Chinese paintings on panels, exquisitely drawn and tinted, which harmonise well with the delicate satinwood of which the cabinet is made. The supports are simply turned and the whole design is free from all unnecessary ornament and carving which form so large and so expensive an item in most modern furniture. Such a cabinet as this made in American walnut or mahogany would cost about £16". This reflects the economies made possible by machine assisted production. The larger makers were not slow to realise that the new mode lent itself to mechanisation and it was probably in the 1870s that furniture was first purposely designed with a view to machine production.

The inexpensive nature of the new style must certainly have helped to promote its growth as the *Building News* pointed out in 1881: "In the production of cheap furniture of artistic design Messrs. Jackson & Graham, among other manufacturers, have endeavoured to meet the requirements of those who cannot afford to furnish their houses in Italian, French or Chippendale furniture. They are making some very excellent buffets and other furniture of exceedingly simple design, the lines of the framework being relieved by plain flutings and moulded work. . . suites of bedroom furniture, made in pine and stained green

Plate 90. Bedroom suite designed by Maurice B. Adams, FRIBA, mid-1880s. Note architectural details and how all items were raised so that space underneath could be kept clean, a current preoccupation in fever-ridden times.

with black mouldings; some excellent painted bedroom furniture all produced by machinery at reasonable cost."[10] Similarly in 1882 it commended the bedroom suite in Plate 90 designed by Maurice B. Adams and made by Robertson & Sons of Alnwick: "The constructive lines are all of the most simple character and are thus designed with the idea of the work being largely executed by the aid of machinery."[11]

Plate 91. Edis inspired bedroom 'Fitments' by Jackson and Graham exhibited at the Health Exhibition 1884. Woodwork white, curtains and upholstery terracotta. Building News, 1884.

Plate 92. 'Combination Buffet and Cabinet for Dining Room' designed as part of a fitted scheme by Robert Edis, in his book Healthy Furniture and Decoration, *1884.*

FITTED FURNITURE

Edis, like many thinking people at that time when typhoid, cholera and a variety of fevers still regularly took toll of many lives, was greatly concerned with the health hazards created by furnishings. Professor Huxley preached against the dangers in dust and a Dr. Richardson on "the unhealthy association of carpets and certain draperies" whilst Rhoda Garrett, who was herself to die of typhoid at the age of forty, had stressed the need for the very minimum of furniture in bedrooms "so as to ensure a free circulation of air". Edis insisted that chests of drawers unless solid to the ground "... should stand well above the floor on strong or plainly turned legs so as to be easily movable and to allow the space under being thoroughly cleaned and dusted". It was his obsession with the dangers of dust that could gather on the tops of cupboards and wardrobes that led Edis to pioneer fitted furniture schemes as in Plate 91 of a bedroom by Jackson & Graham at the International Health Exhibition held in London in 1884. "The wardrobe accommodation was extended to the ceiling by a series of lockers ranging over the fixed chests of drawers and hanging presses", and there were useful cupboards and drawers on either side of the fire instead of merely decorative pilasters. This Ruskinian concept "fitted for a place and subordinated to a purpose" also inspired Edis' fitted dining room seen in Plate 92. Fitted furniture schemes were pronounced by *The Cabinet Maker* "a new departure in the history of house furnishing".[12]

THE SUSSEX RUSH-SEATED CHAIRS

MORRIS AND COMPANY

449 OXFORD STREET, LONDON, W.

"ROSSETTI" ARM-CHAIR.
IN BLACK, 10/6.

SUSSEX CORNER CHAIR.
IN BLACK, 10/6.

SUSSEX SINGLE CHAIR.
IN BLACK, 7/-

SUSSEX ARM-CHAIR.
IN BLACK, 9/6.

ROUND-SEAT CHAIR.
IN BLACK, 10/6.

SUSSEX SETTEE, 4 FT. 6 IN. LONG.
IN BLACK, 35/-.

ROUND SEAT PIANO CHAIR.
IN BLACK, 10/6.

"Of all the specific minor improvements in common household objects due to Morris, the rush-bottomed Sussex chair perhaps takes the first place. It was not his own invention, but was copied with trifling improvements from an old chair of village manufacture picked up in Sussex. With or without modification it has been taken up by all the modern furniture manufacturers, and is in almost universal use. But the Morris pattern of the later type (there were two) still excels all others in simplicity and elegance of proportion."

"Life of William Morris" : By Prof. J. W. Mackail.

Plate 93. These rush seated chairs are thought to have been sold by Morris and Co. from c.1865. Ford Madox Brown apparently persuaded the firm to make them and Rossetti was very involved. This advertisement is post-1899.

Plate 94. Anglo-Japanese rush seat furniture by Benjamin North and Sons, High Wycombe.
Cabinet Maker, June 1881.

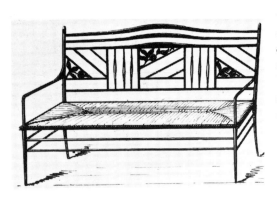

RUSH SEATED FURNITURE

Another feature of the time was the new found respectability of the rush seated chair as seen in Plate 93. Morris and Co. had been selling them since 1865. Mrs. Loftie, Mrs. Orrinsmith and Mrs. Haweis, that influential trio of taste-moulders, all commended them. "Ever since William Morris and Robert Edis drew attention to the advantages of rush seated chairs fashion has set in that direction." Plate 94, of distinctly Anglo-Japanese rush seated furniture by Benjamin North in "dull black or ebonized or American walnut or mahogany or other", shows High Wycombe responding to fashion's challenge. Edis' championing of them was saluted in this verse in *The World* in 1883:

Now blessings on your trusty tongue, good Mr. Edis be
Who've dared to show that Use with Beauty need not disagree
To fling your gage at Folly's feet and live an honest Briton
Maintain your firm conviction that all chairs were meant to sit on.

But the reviewer of the Artizan's Model Dwellings Furnishings at the New Art Museum, Manchester, in 1884 rightly questioned the Morris rush seated settee, Plate 93: "... has it the receptive qualities calculated to give comfort to the couch seeking labourer?" It is indeed surprising that these chairs were so popular. Perhaps Edis like Morris rarely felt the need to sit in comfort and dedicated aesthetes were prepared to put up with discomfort in the quest for the artistic. At least these chairs were inexpensive.

OTHER ORIGINAL WORK

There was a limited amount of unusual furniture inspired not, as in Chapter 3, by contemporary Cairo, but by the Egypt of the Pharaohs. Egyptian artefacts, including items recently excavated from tombs at Thebes, had received considerable publicity at the 1862 Exhibition. One designer they influenced was the very far-sighted Christopher Dresser whose sofa, c.1880, Plate 95, is decorated with ancient Egyptian forms. The oak and pine wardrobe, Plate 96, has hieroglyphics, Egyptian figures and banded reeded columns. Plate 97 shows other seat and couch designs by Dresser and Plate 98 shows his characteristic concern to give extra support to the backs of seats. Dresser ran the Art Furnishers Alliance in Bond Street from 1880-83. The attendants were robed in 'aesthetic costumes in demure art colours' as in Plate 99.

Plate 95. Mahogany sofa, carved and inlaid with ivory, ebony and other woods, designed by Christopher Dresser for Bushloe House, Leicestershire, c.1880. Courtesy Victoria and Albert Museum.

Plate 96. Oak and pine wardrobe with Egyptian painted decoration and tiles, undocumented, c.1880?
Courtesy Victoria and Albert Museum.

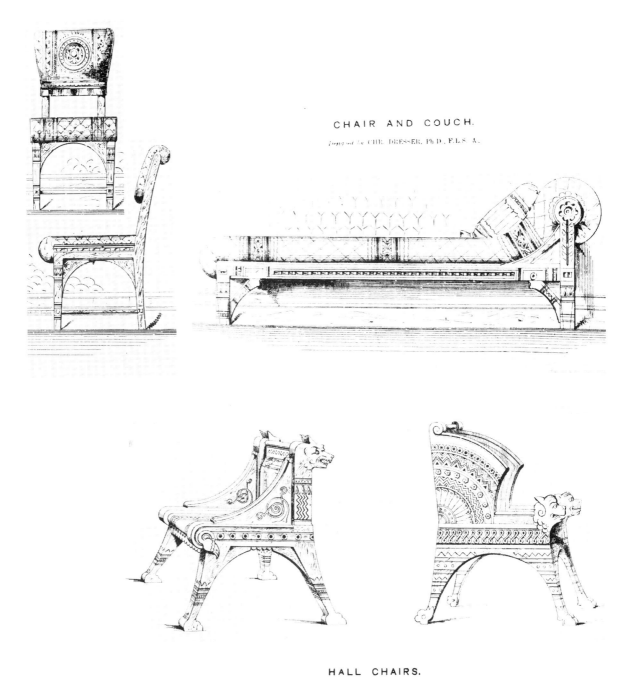

CHAIR AND COUCH.

Designed by CHR. DRESSER, Ph.D., F.L.S., &c.

HALL CHAIRS.

Designed by CHR. DRESSER. Ph.D., F.L.S , &c.

Plate 97. Chair and couch and hall chairs designed by Christopher Dresser, appeared in Furniture Gazette, *January and February 1880.*

Plate 98. Lightweight painted chair with strengthened back sold in Dresser's Art Furnishers Alliance shop, 157 New Bond Street, 1880-83.

The stool in Plate 100, inspired by tomb furniture, was sold by Liberty & Co. from c.1884, when it was Registered No. 16674.

But the Egyptian influence was not widespread, unless the very much used incised ring decoration was inspired by the incisions on the legs of the Egyptian stool exhibited at the 1862 Exhibition.

Although the campaign for simplicity had been taken up by some of the best firms in the trade, general production was, of course, still dominated by repro pastiches and over decoration. In his annual review of 'West End Windows' in December 1886 the editor of *The Cabinet Maker* concluded: "The refined side of modern English furniture . . . is distinguished by a restraint which is as rare as it is excellent . . . the art teaching of the last decade has not been altogether in vain . . . but . . . the love of shams was it seems only scotched and not killed by the crusade of those who so strenuously exposed the make-believes and uglinesses of our trade and we shall want another Peter the Hermit in the shape of a new Eastlake or Talbert to wage war once again."

That crusade is the subject of Chapter 5.

Footnotes

1. *Ornamental Interiors*, 1887
2. The book developed from an article in the *Cornhill Magazine*, March 1864, and went into four editions in ten years. It was very influential in the U.S.
3. *Examples of Ancient and Modern Furniture*, 1876.
4. *Cabinet Maker*, Vol. 3, p.75, October 2, 1882.
5. *Building News*, Vol. 15, pp.869-70, December 24, 1868.
6. J. Moyr Smith, *Ornamental Interiors*, 1887.
7. The most relevant of these are: W.J. Loftie, *A Plea for Art in the House*, 1876; R. & A. Garrett, *Suggestions for House Decoration*, 1877; Mrs Orrinsmith, *The Drawing Room*, 1877; Mrs Loftie, *The Dining Room*, 1878.
8. W. Hamilton, *The Aesthetic Movement in England*, 1882, gives an interesting contemporary account.
9. *Cabinet Maker*, Vol. 2, p.175, March 1, 1882.
10. *Building News*, Vol. 41, p.319, September 9, 1881.
11. *Building News*, Vol. 42, p.634, May 26, 1882.
12. *Cabinet Maker*, Vol. 5, p.1, July 1884.

Plate 99. Attendant in Art Furnishers Alliance wearing "greenery-yallery" dress, ruby sash and mob cap "to harmonize".

Plate 100. Liberty Thebes stool, registered No. 16674, in 1884. They were available in oak or mahogany, price 17s. 6d. (in 1907).

CHAPTER 5

Progressive Furniture c.1885-1910

Although the majority of the trade probably was busy with repro or over be-spindled and bracketed art furniture there were by the early 1880s some firms offering relatively simple but well proportioned, honestly made furniture as, for example in Plates 89 and 101. The battle had been won on a narrow front through the influence of Eastlake, the designs of Talbert and Collcutt and others and by the initiative of Collinson and Lock and other forward looking firms. A new generation of designers was able to advance from that liberated position. The new men: Mackmurdo, Gimson, Voysey, Walton, Mackintosh, Ellwood, Baillie Scott and others have been seen as isolated pillars of inspiration suddenly bursting in with enlightenment but, in fact, they came in on the tide of that already well established crusade for more honest and rational furniture. Because it had made some headway they could proceed, less encumbered by the past, to seek new forms and methods and ravishments.

One of the most original thinkers of the time was Christopher Dresser who worked in many modes from Egyptian to gothic but the simple chair in Plate 98 shows his back to essentials approach. It was sold in his Art Furnishers Alliance shop in Old Bond Street (1880-83). But after this closed he seems to have designed mainly ceramics, metalwork and wallpapers instead of the needed new furniture.

Perhaps the most influential of the new generation was Arthur Heygate Mackmurdo (1851-1942) who wrote in 1883 "We should study not steal our art, passing all through the alembic of our own mind." The previous year he had helped to found The Century Guild whose high aim was to "render all branches of art the sphere no longer of the tradesman but of the artist and to restore building, decoration and the applied arts to their rightful place besides painting and sculpture." This contempt for 'the trade' is a regrettable trait found in too many of the reformers. Despite their brilliance Mackmurdo, William Morris, Walter Crane and others were so blinkered by their own views that they were sometimes querulously unbalanced and given to childishly over-simplified judgements. Because some firms produced shoddy, ugly, over decorated goods these critics condemned the whole trade and created an erroneous impression that good craftsmanship was not available. Even *The Artist* considered Mackmurdo's language about the trade "shockingly improper".

Plate 101. A selection exhibited at The First Furniture Trade Annual Exhibition, 1881. Note the straight lines and architectural 'trim' of these items. Furniture Gazette.

Plate 103, right. More Mackmurdo exhibits at the Inventions Exhibition. The legs, each with four shafts, were a much copied feature. From Cabinet Maker, *Vol. 6, p.32, July 1885.*

Plate 102. The architectural music room settle designed by Mackmurdo and exhibited on the Century Guild stand at Inventions Exhibition, 1885. The widely projecting cornice was a feature taken up by many later designers. Cabinet Maker, *Vol. 6, July 1885.*

Plate 104. Tall chair designed by Mackmurdo, made by E. Goodall and Co., Manchester and shown at the 'Shipperies' Exhibition, 1886. Courtesy Victoria and Albert Museum.

Plates 102 and 103 show some of the first of Mackmurdo's furniture as exhibited at the Inventions Exhibition in 1885. Heavy cornices were already a common feature of trade furniture (Plate 86) in the Victorian Queen Anne manner but, perhaps, the sheer size and height of this settle emphasised and spread the idea of the tall corniced piece. Certainly the feature was to be much used by the new designers.

This tall chair, Plate 104, which Mackmurdo exhibited on the Century Guild's stand at the 'Shipperies' Exhibition in Liverpool in 1886, may well have been the inspiration for the many tall chairs which were to be such a feature of progressive furniture in the 90s. Why so many of the designers were obsessed by height is not clear but one reasonable explanation may be that their eyes had become attuned to attenuated shapes through familiarity with Japanese prints and pictures which had been so much on view since the 70s. The chair was condemned at the time for its "sharp projecting, elbow splitting cornice," and the *Cabinet Maker* grumbled that the irrational cornice would leave a passer-by "winded and wounded." He complained, with more justification, about the widely projecting, "chopper like caps" on the table legs in Plate 103 being well placed to catch the knees. But this type of flat projection (again in Plate 105) and legs formed, as here, by four shafts were features taken up by later designers.

Obviously this furniture by Mackmurdo was in great contrast to the then fashionable art furniture (Plates 76 to 79), as the *Journal of Decorative Arts* explained in November 1887, because of its "Simplicity and largeness of design . . . No frittering away of interest in a multitude of small spindles, recesses and shelves . . . The first impression is one of Boldness but this is due no doubt to the mental dissipation we have indulged in of late . . . with . . . a multitude of small spaces and re-dundancy of detail . . . The whole exhibit [Manchester Jubilee Exhibition 1887] is important as indicating the tendency and drift of taste in the next few years." Mackmurdo's furniture was made by Wilkinson & Son, Old Bond Street, Collinson & Lock and Goodall & Co, Manchester and could be seen there and at his office, 28 Southampton Street, WC1. He thought "those workers whose aims seem to be most nearly in accord with us are Rhoda (d.1883) and Agnes Garrett and J. Aldam Heaton."[1] It is interesting that his

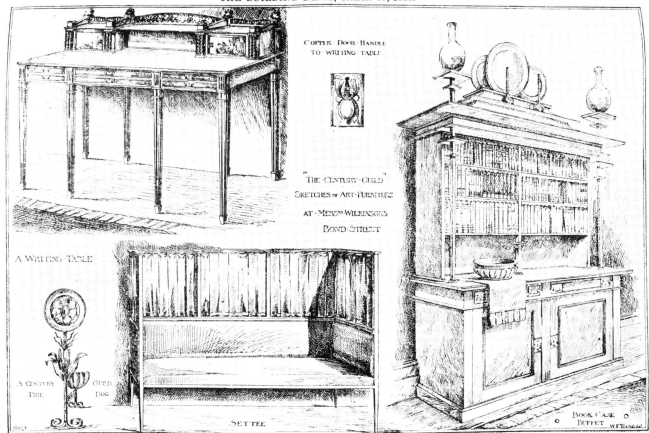

Plate 105. More Mackmurdo items exhibited by the Century Guild and made by Wilkinsons of Bond Street, 1888. Note the projections and cornice on the bookcase-buffet. From Building News, *March 30, 1888.*

furniture which, it must be admitted, was not entrancingly attractive, should have been so influential. Mackmurdo was a designer's designer.

There were many other exhibitions in the 80s including, from 1881, The Annual Furniture Trade Exhibitions, Plate 101. In 1882 there was the Fine Arts and Industries Exhibition in Manchester where Morris & Co. showed a very heavy walnut cabinet "somewhat incongruous with its angular cornice, serpentine shelves and very massive mouldings" but it was welcomed as a "sort of solid protest against many deal lined, flimsy, gaudily be-dizered contemporaries." Morris himself, according to his chief designer, George Jack, always seemed "somewhat indifferent about this (furniture) branch of his business and did nothing in this way himself."[2] Perhaps he was haunted by memories of the first seat he designed for his rooms in Bloomsbury as, when delivered, he found it occupied one third of the area of the floor.

At the New Art Museum Exhibition in Queen's Park, Manchester, in 1884 Morris & Co. furnished an 'Artizan's Model Dwelling' (Plate 106). This included a very simple wash-stand, designed by W.A.S. Benson, with splayed sides, the forerunner of many of this shape.[3]

Plate 106. Wash-stand by Morris and Co. in the Artizan's Model Dwellings Furnishings Exhibition, the New Art Museum, Manchester, 1884, designed by W.A.S. Benson. Note the splayed sides. From Cabinet Maker, *Vol. 5, p.122.*

Plate 107. Mahogany secretaire-bookcase by Graham and Banks: "here we have the rich tones of the mahogany relieved by inlay of the broad decorative character that has been cultivated of late by one or two of our leading manufacturers." Cabinet Maker, January 1899.

Another Morris & Co. exhibit was a sideboard at the Manchester Jubilee Exhibition, 1887. Designed by George Jack but made by someone else its sides were raised well above board level and there were hefty tall candelabrum posts at the front corners. It is a remote connection but were these perhaps inspired by memories of Godwin's great upward projections on the wardrobe in Plate 72? A feature of the sideboard much taken up by later designers was the black and white chequered stringing which ran up the posts and across the front. This was then referred to as 'tarsia work'.[4] But, as someone remarked at the time "it requires a long purse to live up to the higher phases of Morrisean taste" and this sideboard seems to have remained unsold. It was exhibited again at the first Arts and Crafts Exhibition Society show in 1888.

That Society, formed as a protest against industrialism and to honour and encourage craftsmanship, contained very gifted men including some of the most progressive of the new generation of furniture designers and it is usually assumed that the Society's exhibitions had great influence. But the effect these exhibitions had on furniture design seems to have been considerably over estimated. At the first Arts and Crafts Exhibition at the New Gallery in 1888 there was very little furniture and Lewis F. Day's imposing cabinet the only really notable piece. This is in the Victoria and Albert Museum and illustrated in Elizabeth Aslin's *Nineteenth Century English Furniture*.

Nor was the Society's second exhibition in 1889 remarkable for advanced furniture designs. There was a large settle designed by Walter Crane and painted with a feeble example of worse verse and a very finely executed enclosed writing table by George Jack "like an exaggerated inlaid, giant tea caddy on a clumsy stand." Of the third exhibition in 1890 *The Builder* reported "there is some falling off in the success of these exhibitions . . . the private view was by no means crowded and the rooms have been very sparsely attended since".[5] The exhibitions took place triennially after this and many exhibits were more notable for fine craftsmanship than for their advanced design.

The 1899 Exhibition did contain more progressive pieces by Voysey and Baillie Scott but, in that year, *The Artist* reported, after an

Plate 108. Sideboards by Bath Cabinet Makers' Co. The left in medium mahogany with copper mounts, the other in fumed oak with copper mounts and stained green door panels in the upper part. From special issue of Cabinet Maker, March 1899.

interview with George Jack, a founder member of the Society: "Mr Jack thinks the Arts and Crafts exhibitions chiefly of use as a shop affording exhibitors the chance of legitimate advertisement . . . Beyond that the influence it exerts on manufacturers he thinks is small . . . he feels that some men are disposed to attach too much importance to the work done and the influence of the triennial show." He regretted too that often items did not sell because of the inevitably high price of hand craftsmanship.[6] By 1906 *The Studio* judged ". . . it is lamentably certain that the advance which one had every right to expect has not taken place, the Society still remains where it was."

Nevertheless the Society had value in enabling members to meet and influence each other; and it had influence through the publicity it received from the new and internationally read *Studio* magazine after 1893. No doubt some of the designers received commissions because of publicity in it.

Who then were the new men? Ernest Gimson, Sidney and Ernest Barnsley, Charles Voysey and Makay Hugh Baillie Scott are the best known of the Arts and Crafts Exhibition Society members, and George Walton and Charles Rennie Mackintosh of the rest, but there were a good many gifted designers working on their own and for the trade. Few are known and most have as yet received too little notice. So many of the designers were contemporaries that it is very difficult to discover who did what first and who influenced whom. So much of their furniture remains yet to be discovered that many of the illustrations have had to be taken from old photographs and from line drawings in contemporary magazines.

It is probably clearest to treat each designer separately but first it will be useful to look at the characteristics of some of this 'progressive' furniture of the 1890s. Some of the features: the cut out shapes, long important hinges and ring handles, the revealed construction and use of solid timber, the splayed sides, plank legs and inscribed mottoes had all been common at least since Eastlake-Talbert times. But the shapes of the cut through work were new with hearts and spades predominating. The designs of the hinges were new and these and the metal mounts were important features often in copper and involving sinuous lines. There is a new involvement with the triangle and with tulip shapes. Mackmurdo's high cornices inspired a long line of overhanging horizontals on cabinets, wardrobes and many items, whilst his powerful verticals were echoed in many supporting shafts and all too many functionless projections. Plate 128.

Dark and light chequered stringing came to be a very common feature, almost a hall-mark of the period. Inlay and marquetry were important ingredients in the work of some designers, notably in early Gimson pieces and a bolder, freer type of marquetry was employed particularly by Graham and Banks, J.S. Henry and Bath Cabinet Makers (Plates 107 and 108). Other features and the really original work of progressive designers will appear in later plates.

The adjective 'progressive', incidentally, was little used at the time but is, in fact, more indicative and relevant than the names then used. Of these 'British New Art' which headed Plate 109 drawn in 1904, is inadequate because the word 'new' cannot in English be permanently annexed by any past period. The now often used name 'Arts and Crafts' is inaccurate as much of the original work did not stem from that Society. As for the title 'l'art nouveau', it was then applied to

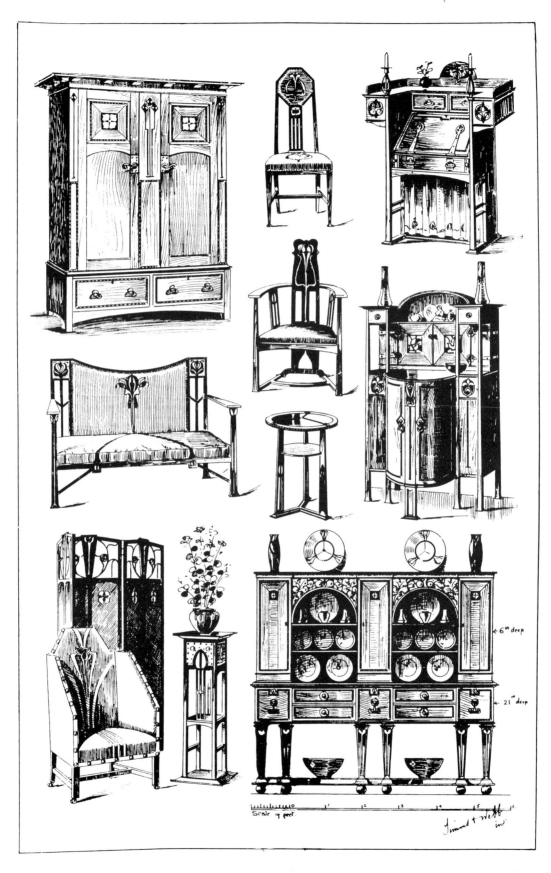

Plate 109. Plate 'British New Art' from Timms and Webb, Thirty Five Styles of Furniture, *1904.*

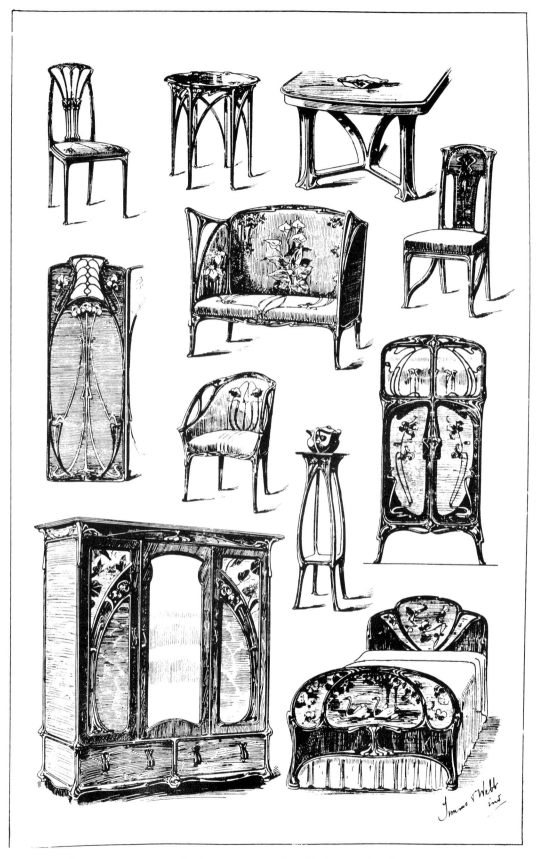

Plate 110. Plate 'L'Art Nouveau', from Timms and Webb, Thirty Five Styles of Furniture, *1904. These mainly sketched from exhibits at the Paris Exhibition of 1900.*

contemporary French and other continental work with essentially curvaceous forms as in Plate 110. That and Plate 109 well illustrate the obvious differences between French and British work then so that, although each influenced the other and the whiplash motif and sinuous forms did feature in British decorative arts then, it is obvious from these plates that the title 'art nouveau' cannot usefully be applied to the furniture of both and should be reserved for the French productions. Charles Handley Read wrote well of the differences: "The English furniture . . . is always symmetrical in overall shape. None is marked by its plasticity; its structural members never seem about to melt or deliquesce compared with the 'attenuated linearity' of work by Galle, Gaillard and others where structure and decoration including hinges and handles blend in a plastic, indivisible unity."[7] Those here who did not like the French forms referred to the style as 'the Squirm' and when the South Kensington Museum foresightedly bought, with the Donaldson Bequest, a selection of the French art nouveau furniture

Plate 111. *J.S. Henry advertisement from* Cabinet Maker, *June 1896.*

Plate 113. *Three items exhibited by J.S. Henry at Brussels Exhibition, 1897. Note the very high backed chair.* Cabinet Maker, *September 1897.*

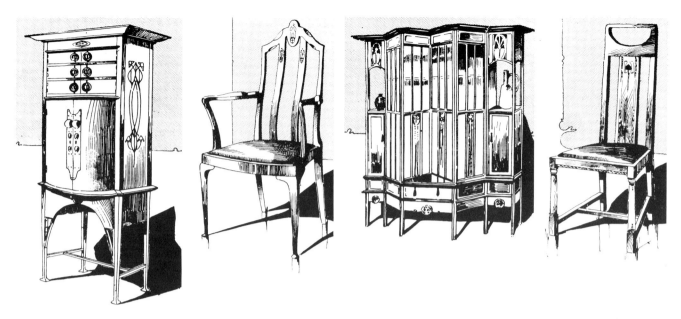

Plate 114. Items exhibited by J.S. Henry at an Exhibition in the Dublin Museum, 1905. From Cabinet Maker, August 26, 1905. Note the more traditional chair.

Plate 115. Cabinet, what-not and un-usually staid chair by J.S. Henry ex-hibited in Paris Exhibition, 1900. The Artist, Vol. 29, September 1900.

exhibited at the 1900 Paris Exhibition, Walter Crane, President of the Arts and Crafts Exhibition Society, led the protest against this writing to *The Times*: "This work is neither right in principle nor does it evince a proper regard for the materials employed."

The only other much used name at the time was 'Quaint'. This word had advanced from its accepted meaning in 1880 when Louis Sullivan described his Chicago Auditorium Building with its "tangle of tendrils, scalloped leaves and tortuous marine growths" as "in the Quaint Style". But, obviously, its true meaning "uncommon in appearance but attractive, especially having an old fashioned prettiness or daintiness" renders it inapplicable as a name for original furniture. As the word appeared in many advertisements for feebly designed pieces encumbered with curly laths and other irrelevances, poor quality new productions of that time have come to be labelled 'commercial quaint'. This is unfortunate and furniture historians should beware using the word commercial in a solely derogatory sense. All furniture, except DIY and the often quirky products of a few querulous architects, is 'commercial'. Furniture making is a commercial activity.

As then the four other names are all inadequate, the term 'Progressive', still having its freshly minted meaning of something "characterised by moving onwards" seems relevant and acceptable. The most interesting of the new furniture did appear to be part of a forward looking movement. It was mainly furniture most suited to houses in the country or garden city. Not enough was designed for the smart town house.

It would be difficult to find a more accurate statement of the aims of most of the new designers than that which had appeared in a letter in the *Furniture Gazette* in 1880. It purported to be [prophetically?] from a correspondent in Glasgow but it sounds so like the views of the then new editor, Christopher Dresser, that it seems reasonable to suggest that perhaps it was, with editor's licence, 'planted' by him. The writer, the letter said, ". . . has waited and wished for the time to come when designers would disencumber their minds of all that pertains to this,

Plate 116. Mahogany cabinet with very sophisticated detail labelled J.S. Henry.
Courtesy Victoria and Albert Museum.

that or other style and go to work in a straight forward and self reliant manner, giving some thought to the purpose for which various pieces of furniture are required; the nature of the material of which they are to be made, the soundest and most economical methods of construction, the proportion of parts one to another and the effect when viewed as a whole, not forgetting the most legitimate way of ornamenting and finishing the work that they may be called upon to design."

THE PROGRESSIVE DESIGNERS

So much remains to be discovered about the following and other, as yet unknown, designers that this can only be a report of work in progress. They are listed roughly in order of their arrival before the public. Preference has been given to plates little known or rarely illustrated pieces.

Readers should consult Elizabeth Aslin's very valuable *19th century English Furniture* for plates of important museum items. *Modern British Domestic Architecture and Decoration*, 1901, referred to hereafter as MBDAD, illustrates other items by the designers.

A map showing the position of these men would have several dots in Glasgow and one in Arbroath, several in the Cotswolds, one in Cumberland, one in Bedford and one or two in Manchester and a good many in London. Some like Arthur Simpson in Kendal worked in isolation, some, like Mackintosh, George Walton and the McNairs, knew and influenced each other as did the Barnsleys and Gimson in the Cotswolds, whilst most worked in the hurly-burly of London helping the trade "to keep pace with the present quick march of fashion and the absolute necessity to have something new."

When an interesting new piece is found it is all too tempting to try to attribute it to one of the well known names but it should be remembered that striking and attractive features once seen were eagerly adopted in the prevailing search for novelty. Firms did not often give the names of designers of their products. For example, the table by Ellwood with pierced plank legs in J.S. Henry's drawing room, Plate 150, appears in the c.1910 catalogue of Norman and Stacey, Plate 220.

THE FIRM OF MORRIS AND CO. 1861-c.1905

They do not exactly fit here but must be included. Philip Webb and W.A.S. Benson designed for them before George Jack.

Their products fall into three main categories:

1. The inexpensive rush seated 'Sussex' and other cane seated chairs.
2. Plainish items in current fashion, e.g. the whatnot in Plate 226.
3. Elaborate painted and/or inlaid cabinets, e.g. Plate 141. They were expensive — a secretaire with foliage inlay 98 guineas and "a handsome inlaid cabinet of Italian walnut 6 feet by 7 feet three inches, £170."

JOHN SOLLIE HENRY in business 1880 — after 1910

Plates 109, 111, 113-116 show advanced designs by J.S. Henry's firm but the designers are as yet unknown. From 1880 when he started business Henry had concentrated on the new and unusual. The *Cabinet Maker* of October 1895 referred to the "vast number of entirely novel and artistic designs which he has put on the market ... The selection of goods now on show at 287-89 Old Street E.C. bristles with novelty ... in shape from the most severe to the most fanciful." George Ellwood

Plate 117. A robust cupboard with revealed construction in oak. Designed by Ernest Gimson and made in his Daneway workshop, Sapperton.
Courtesy The Shire Museum, Leicester.

was designing for the firm around 1900 but who else? Henry described himself as a designer. Plate 113 shows the very tall chair, well pre-Mackintosh, that Henry exhibited in Brussels in 1897.

ERNEST BARNSLEY 1863-1926

He met William Morris whilst studying in an architect's office in Leicester. As a result he went to work for J.D. Sedding next door to the showrooms of Morris & Co., in Oxford Street. He made himself very familiar with all the processes and skills of wood craftsmanship but was not primarily a craftsman himself. He was one of the founders of Kenton and Co. in 1890. In this little company five designers, as a sideline, employed four or five cabinet makers. They held a successful exhibition at Barnard's Inn but the company folded in 1892 for lack of capital. Gimson designed some very original pieces, for example the inlaid cabinet exhibited at the Arts and Crafts Exhibition, 1890. Later Gimson and the Barnsley brothers moved to Gloucestershire and in 1903 were established in Sapperton. Gimson at Daneway House had very able assistants: Ernest Smith, Henry Davoll, Fred Gardiner and Percy (Hugh) Burchett and later a very gifted foreman, Peter Waals.

The Gimson characteristics were through dovetail joints, black and white inlay, hand wrought handles, inlaid escutcheons, unstained, unpolished oak, through mortise and tenon joints with dowels showing, gouge decoration with fielded panels and handles as part of the design. His mahogany, walnut and ebony pieces were polished with white French polish, rubbed down with glass paper and waxed. He had a great gift for recognising the potential of materials. Lethaby wrote: "Every piece was thought out definitely for particular picked wood and for clearly understood ways of workmanship and his supervision was so constant and thorough that the design was changed in process of making as the materials and working might suggest."[8] (Plates 117 and 118.) The Leicester Museum has a selection of his work. There are important examples in the Victoria and Albert Museum and its high quality can be seen in the stalls in the St. Andrew's Chapel, Westminster Cathedral, S.W.1. After his death Peter Waals continued the high level of production, Plate 119.

SIDNEY BARNSLEY 1865-1926

Another architect founder of Kenton and Co. and another architect turned designer craftsman, he worked at the bench mainly in the Cotswolds from 1895-1924. His robust totally handcrafted work was dubbed "the butter tub and carpenter's bench style." Plates 120 and 121.

ERNEST BARNSLEY 1863-1926

A practising architect he made furniture mainly only for himself. He also was a founder of Kenton and Co. and moved to Sapperton. Plate 122.

WILLIAM LETHABY 1857-1931

Principal of the Central School of Arts and Crafts, and one of the founders of Kenton and Co., he was not primarily a furniture designer but he did design for Marsh, Jones and Cribb and J.P. White. One of his best known pieces (see Aslin) was the sideboard for Melsetter House, Hoy, Orkney, c.1900.

Plate 118. A more sophisticated cabinet with bone inlay, designed by Gimson and made in his Daneway Workshop.
Courtesy The Shire Museum, Leicester.

Plate 119. Wardrobe by Peter Waals. In walnut with ebony and holly raised bandings on block chamfered trestle supports. Mounts hand wrought in brass. Central doors applied with raised square and octagonal panels.
Courtesy Sotheby's Belgravia.

Plate 122. Walnut desk by Ernest Barnsley. The drawer pedestals are slightly bowed. Monogrammed and incised on back OP, 3E9, 1909. 4ft. 5½in. wide.
Courtesy Sotheby's Belgravia.

GEORGE JACK

He exhibited a mahogany cabinet and a sideboard at the first Arts and Crafts Exhibition, 1888. He designed for Morris & Co. for many years, certainly from 1887. Many elaborate marquetry items were designed by him. He was a very skilled carver but whether also an inlayer is not clear.[9]

Frederick Litchfield in his *Illustrated History of Furniture*, 1892, listed the following regular contributors of furniture designs to the trade journals:

J.W. Bliss
R.A. Briggs, ARIBA
H.L. Gill
Bertram Goodhue
Ernest George and Peto
A. Jonquet
Felix Lenoir
Lethaby
Wilbert Rattray
Stenhouse
John Turner
Frank Ward
A.H. Wolf
W. Timms
Webb

But most of these probably did not design progressive furniture.

GEORGE WALTON 1867-1933, Architect

He attended evening classes at the Glasgow School of Art and was still a bank accountant when he accepted a decorative commission for a new smoking room for one of Miss Cranston's tea rooms.

Plate 120. A robust dresser with revealed construction by Sidney Barnsley. Exhibited 1903. From the Cabinet Maker *which dubbed it the "butter-tub-and-carpenter's-bench-style ... the shelves supported (!) by what resembles more than anything else a tape-worm in convulsions after a good strong dose of male-fern."*

Plate 121. Oak dresser by Sidney Barnsley. Note the through tenons.

Plate 123. Sideboard by George Walton. From British Homes for Today, *1904.*

Plate 124. Wash-stand and toilet table by George Walton. From Modern British Domestic Architecture and Decoration, 1901.

Plate 125. Sidetable with bold inlay by George Walton.

1888	He set up in Glasgow as 'George Walton and Co., Ecclesiastical and House Decorators'.
1890	He exhibited at the Arts and Crafts Exhibition in London.
1897	Opened a business in London and in 1898 one in York.
1897-1902	He designed shop fronts and interiors and furniture for Kodak in Brussels, Glasgow, Milan, Moscow, Vienna and five London branches.
1901	He designed The Leys, Elstreet and Elmbank, York and some furniture for each and furniture for a billiard room for Miss Cranston. The chairs had broad flat arms, cut-through hearts in the centre of the curved, almost triangular backs.
1907-10	He designed The White House, Shiplake, and some of its furniture. Some of his work is very elegant, as in Plate 123, and some tallish caned chairs with slim outward curving legs. He favoured tall galleries round chests and dressing tables. Plate 124. He sometimes used a little bold geometrical inlay. Plate 125. As Walton was in business for more than twenty years there must be a good deal of his furniture about. Plate 126.

CHARLES FRANCIS ANNESLEY VOYSEY 1857-1941, Architect

Voysey studied architecture under Seddon and Davey and was designing houses from the late 1880s. One of his earliest furniture designs in the RIBA Collection is pencil dated 1891 and has two of his most characteristic features: hearts punched out of the ends and long strap hinges. His best known design is the writing desk made for him by

Plate 126. Walnut display cabinet by George Walton with stylised twist ribbon mouldings, c.1905.

Plate 128. Writing table and chair exhibited by C.F.A. Voysey in British Section at International Exhibition in Turin, 1902. From Cabinet Maker, March 1903.

Plate 127. Writing desk, oak with copper hinges designed by C.F.A. Voysey 1896, made by W.H. Tingey. Voysey paid special attention to the designing of metal mounts.
Courtesy Victoria and Albert Museum.

W.H. Tingey in 1896. Plate 127. The influence of Mackmurdo is obvious. This sophisticated desk shows the enterprising way Voysey employed metalwork. He designed a whole range of hinges, handles, lock plates, etc. Some of the instructions on his drawings are very much in the Eastlake-Talbert tradition as, for example, "to be left free from stain or polish" and "oak table, no nails or screws to be used in construction."

Plate 128 shows the writing table and chair that Voysey exhibited at the International Exhibition in Turin in 1902. The Mackmurdian verticals seem distinctly irrelevant. A critic then wrote: "If Mr Voysey in designing a writing table had set himself to produce an article that would furnish possibilities of the maximum of knocks to one's elbows and the minimum of accommodation for books and paper he could hardly have succeeded better, while as for the chair!!!" This stripped down, very basic chair anticipates Rietveld's famous 'red-blue' type by fifteen years. It suggests Voysey's probing, open minded approach but, actually, it is only a simplified version of a studio chair with a flat inclined back exhibited by Arthur Simpson in 1896.[10] The characteristic Voysey chair has a tall back as exhibited in 1899. Plate 129(e).

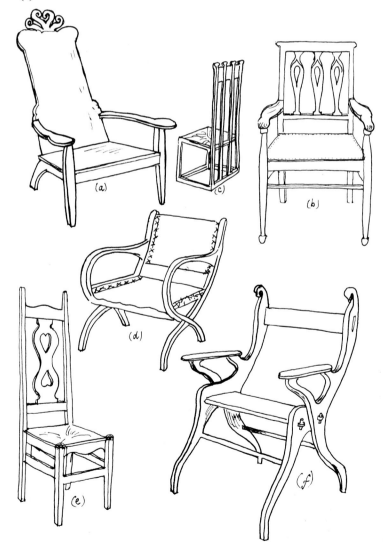

Plate 129. New designs for chairs (a) and (by Arthur Simpson, 1896 and c.1906; (c) G.M. Ellwood, 1899; (d) C.R. Ashbee, 1895; (e) and (f) C.F.A. Voysey, 1899 and c.1897.

The best of his work, like the 'swan' chair in Plate 129(f), has "something of the build of a greyhound with its sensitive grace and its outline, clean vigorous and austere." But many of his later designs as for dressers, wardrobes and dressing tables in the RIBA Collection are very ordinary. Whether his inspiration for furniture flagged or he became more interested in designing for other crafts is not clear. Baillie Scott reviewing Voysey's work for E.J. Horniman's *Garden Corner*, Chelsea, in 1907, obviously had difficulty in raising enthusiasm for it. The work he wrote "consists mainly in the application of serenely sane, practical and rational ideas to home-making . . . His work is true. One may imagine that he has resolved that it shall at least be that." [11] See also plate 130.

The makers' names mentioned on the Voysey drawings are (C.F.) Nielsen and Coo(t?)e and Arthur Simpson is thought to have executed some of his designs. Voysey also designed for J.S. Henry and piano cases for Collard and Collard, Bechstein and the Aeolian Co.

CHARLES RENNIE MACKINTOSH 1868-1928

1893   He left Glasgow School of Art, designed his own furniture, including the Dennistoun cabinet, and worked on private design commissions, e.g. 1894-95 for Gladsmuir.

1894-95 His designs for Guthrie and Wells, the Glasgow cabinet makers, appeared in their catalogue.

1895   'The Four' (Charles and Margaret Mackintosh, Herbert and Frances McNair) exhibited by request at the City of Liège Arts and Crafts Exhibition: thus the first link between Glasgow designers and the Continent was forged and they were publicised by the internationally read *Studio* in 1897.

1896   Invited, for the only time, to exhibit at the Arts and Crafts Society Exhibition, he sent a tall hooded settle with stencilled patterns, a painted canvas back, peacock frieze and metal panels. Four short upper posts on either side supported the overhanging top. He is said to have been influenced by Voysey's work there.

Plate 131. An example of C.R. Mackintosh's total concept furnishing. Here the chairs, which in isolation seem theatrical and affected, look fitting and inevitable. From Cabinet Maker, September 1902.

Plate 132. This chair with box panelled, shaped seat and cylindrical legs was designed by C.R. Mackintosh for the Smoking Room of the Argylle Street Tea Rooms, 1897. Courtesy Sotheby's Belgravia.

1897   Furniture for Miss Cranston's Argylle Tea Rooms: semi circular lath back and ladder back chairs (Plate 132), and dish seated stools.

1897-99 He built the first stage of the Glasgow School of Art.

1900   He furnished a room at the Vienna Secession Exhibition.

1900-1 Furnished the Ingram Street Tea Rooms.

1901   *The Studio* published pictures of his very original Mains Street flat furniture.

1902   He designed the very impressive Scottish section for the first International Exhibition of Modern Decorative Art in Turin. Like Mains Street and Hill House later, his schemes were 'total concepts' with every item related to its position in the decorative scheme. Plate 131.

1903   Furnished the Willow Tea Rooms.

c.1904 Designed furniture for Hill House.

Mackintosh had far more influence on the Continent than in Britain. His work is very original and important but some needs to be seen in the positions for which it was planned. He was primarily an architect, a superb manipulator of space. Some of his furniture — the tall dramatic chairs, for example, were designed to articulate certain spaces and look irrational out of context. Plate 131. His work is widely illustrated and can be studied in several volumes listed in the bibliography.

HERBERT and FRANCES McNAIR

They exhibited together with the Mackintoshes in Liège in 1895 and in the dramatic Scottish section at the Turin Exhibition in 1902. See Plates 134 and 135.

Plate 133. Cabinet with clock designed by C.R. Mackintosh.
Courtesy Victoria and Albert Museum.

Plate 135, right. Study by Frances and Herbert McNair. The frieze is painted on the plaster in tones of red and black. The furniture is painted darkly and the lower parts of the walls are covered with brown paper.

Plate 134. Bedroom by Frances and Herbert McNair. This and 135 from Modern British Domestic Architecture and Decoration, *1901.*

ARTHUR W. SIMPSON, Kendal

He was a consistent exhibitor in the Arts and Crafts Society Exhibitions.

1896   He showed four items including a studio chair in polished walnut with a flat inclined back, arms broadened considerably to hold cups and, what looks in the drawing like, an inclined seat. Plate 129(a). He also exhibited a combination writing table and bookcase which the *Building News* judged "a carefully thought out piece . . . Simplicity being Mr. Simpson's chief aim . . . he has succeeded in imparting interest to his work as well."

1901   He showed, at the Arts and Crafts Exhibition in Leeds, an oak studio chair with "plain sloping back, spacious arms spreading out into flat ends to hold ash trays or cup and saucer, (it) breathes hospitality and comfort."

Simpson stamped some of his work. He is thought to have executed some of Voysey's designs.

AMBROSE HEAL Junior

Of the well established quality furniture making business in Tottenham Court Road, he was apprenticed to a cabinet maker in Warwick and then joined the family firm in 1893. He was soon producing simple furniture like the Newlyn bedroom suite in 1897. *The Studio* noted of Heal's recent style in 1899: "For ornament, a restricted use is made of waggon chamfering, like the traditional decoration of drays, vans and costermongers barrows" . . . and also "plates of handles and also key escutcheons . . . being sunk flush with the surface." The very handsome oak wardrobe Heal displayed at the Paris Exhibition of 1900 was inlaid with pewter and ebony. *The Studio* said of his stand at the Glasgow Exhibition of 1901: "Mr Ambrose Heal aims at maintaining in the leading structural lines simplicity of form relieved by a judicious introduction of ornamental detail in the form of inlays . . . Mr Heal's furniture is rich in effect, yet if compared with the average treatment of furniture of similar character, one cannot fail to be struck not by the wealth of ornament but by its extremely reticent use." Plate 136.

Plate 136. Dressing table in oak and ebony by Heal and Son. Exhibited at the Paris Exhibition, 1900.

108

Heal's commitment of his firm to quality simple furniture especially for bedrooms, was a bold move and must have done much to establish the vogue. His Country Cottage suite in oak consisting of 2ft. 6in. wardrobe, dressing chest of drawers with swing mirror, wash-stand with tiled back and one rush bottomed chair, cost £7 15s. carriage paid in U.K. in 1905.

W.A.S. BENSON

He was designing for Morris and Co. by 1882 but his real talent was for metal work. He was a prolific designer of many forms including electric light fittings. Plate 137.

W. BALDOCK

A designer on the staff of the *Cabinet Maker* in the 1880s and 90s he had plenty of inventive ideas, e.g. the 'Quaint' chairs in Plate 138, 1895.

MAKAY HUGH BAILLIE SCOTT 1865-1945

Baillie Scott is one of the most interesting designers of his generation. An architect, practising in Bedford, interested in all branches of decoration, he was essentially a home-maker not a mere decorator. "The furniture" he wrote "should appear to grow out of the requirements of the room, to represent the finishing touches of a scheme which had its inception when the first stage of the house was laid (and not as an alien importation from the upholsterer of spick and spans) . . . Various kinds of fixed furnishings become of special value in the effect of a room filling the gap between the house and its furniture." Thus many of his schemes involved ingle-nooks and other built in features. Plate 139.

He was a regular contributor to *The Studio* from its early days, often of watercolours of interiors. In 1894 he was writing there of 'The Ideal Suburban House' and in Volume 12 of 'A Small Country House.'

His best known work is that for the Grand Duke and Duchess of Hesse's Palace at Darmstadt in 1898. This depended much on its painted decoration. The interior of the secretaire was painted in white, green and orange on a pale green ground. The music cabinet had vivid interior decoration of inlaid woods and ivory. Plate 140. There was a semi-circular writing chair of a form suggested by a Burne-Jones tapestry panel in dark and light green with rose coloured flower heads. Plate 145(b). Another chair had its seat and tall back of green leather picked out with red and pink and fixed with silvery studs.

About 1898 Scott designed the 'Manxman' piano (Plate 142) and some versions of this were colourfully decorated Darmstadt fashion.

In 1902 J.P. White, the high class joinery firm of the Pygtle Works, Bedford, advertised *A Book of Furniture* designed by M.H. Baillie Scott. Among over eighty items it probably included those in Plate 145. They even opened a shop in Margaret Street, W.1., to retail them in 1903 so a good many must have been sold. There was his Daffodil Dresser, the Carnation Lily Rose cabinet and an oak corner cupboard with two daffodils on the front inlaid with pewter, holly, stained woods and carved in low relief, price £4 15s. These all remain to be discovered. (Plate 145.) An inlaid cabinet by him was described in *The Studio*, in August 1904, as stained dark green bronze with stems of roses set and

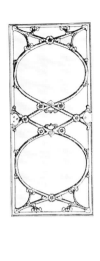

Plate 137. A cabinet with metal work by W.A.S. Benson. Compare with plate 112. From The Artist, *1901.*

Plate 138. Advanced so-called 'quaint' chairs designed by W. Baldock, 1895.

Plate 139. A fitted dining room scheme by M.H. Baillie Scott. Note painted decoration, tall chair and floor level stretchers.
From Modern British Domestic Architecture and Decoration, *1901.*

Plate 140. Music cabinet designed by M.H. Baillie Scott for the Palace at Darmstadt, 1897-8, with vivid interior decoration, white, green and orange on a light green ground.
Courtesy Victoria and Albert Museum.

Plate 142. The Manxman piano designed by M.H. Baillie Scott, 1898. Most examples are plain; this is unusually highly decorated.
Courtesy Victoria and Albert Museum.

Plate 141. Mahogany cabinet elaborately inlaid with ebony and satinwood and painted. Probably designed by George Jack. Made by Morris and Co. for a play, The Crusaders, *in 1891. Possibly Baillie Scott was influenced by this kind of repetitive decoration.*
Courtesy Victoria and Albert Museum.

Plate 143. Settle with pewter and ebonized fruitwood inlay and hinged seat after a design by Baillie Scott. Illustration in The Studio, October 1902.
Courtesy Sotheby's Belgravia.

wrought in pewter and thorns in mother of pearl. "These grey stems with the blue buds and pink roses with their grey, green leaves with touches of bright orange in the fruit of the rose constitute the chief elements in the colour scheme. The interior is lined with sycamore and the parchment tones of this wood afford a well marked contrast to the deepness of the external tones. On this light ground are pink roses and the metal work of the handles which are in brass and copper coloured by a special process to assume permanently prismatic tints."[12] Items as characterful as this can surely be discovered.

GEORGE MONTAGUE ELLWOOD

By 1898 The Artist was already maintaining "Mr Ellwood's charming work is really too well known to require any introduction". Ellwood himself then wrote that although all decorative work is to some extent derivative "we should enter upon our work in the same

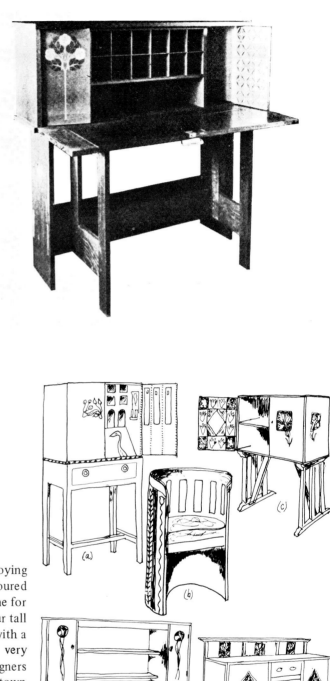

way as the old designers attacked theirs and that is by employing present possibilities to the utmost." [13] Like Baillie Scott he favoured built in fixtures as in Plates 146 and 147. His prize winning scheme for a Bachelor's Room in 1899 included a green stained chair with four tall uprights in the back and floor level stretchers and a writing table with a tall gallery. Around 1900 he was designing for J.S. Henry the very elegant furniture in Plates 148 to 151. He was one of the few designers of the time who provided sophisticated pieces suitable for smart town houses.

In 1908 he advertised as "Ellwood and Sledmere (late with J.S. Henry Ltd), 53 Mortimer Street."

GEORGE LOGAN

He was designing for Wylie and Lochhead of Glasgow c.1900. He exhibited at the Glasgow Exhibition of 1901, in Turin in 1902 and later at the Vienna Secession Exhibition. He was very concerned with colour harmonies and tinted his furniture and used silvery aluminium with enamels as inlays. See his wash-stand with a tall gallery in Plate 152 and tall Mackintosh like chairs in The Studio, Volume 36.

Plate 145. Furniture designed by M.H. Baillie Scott and published in his House and Garden, 1906, but made by J.P. White, The Pygtle Works, Bedford, before then: (a) inlaid secretaire; (b) inlaid chair; (c) the Carnation, Lily, Rose cabinet; (d) the Daffodil dresser; (e) inlaid sideboard.

Plate 146. A fitted furniture scheme for a hall by G.M. Ellwood. The Artist, *Vol. 23.*

Plate 147. A drawing room designed by G.M. Ellwood. From The Artist *Vol. 23.*

Plate 148. Fireplace end of drawing room furnished and decorated for J.S. Henry, Esq., by G.M. Ellwood. Panel in-filling is silk tapestry in deep rich tones of red and orange. Furniture in mahogany upholstered in mauve silk.

Plate 149. Other end of same drawing room. Mahogany furniture inlaid with pewter and various woods, cabinet fittings of copper, chair silk enriched with appliqué design by Mrs. G.M. Ellwood. This and 148 from Modern British Domestic Architecture and Decoration, 1901.

Plate 150. More furniture by G.M. Ellwood for J.S. Henry. Note the pierced plank legs of the table and stool. The table top is of burnished copper.

Plate 151. More furniture by G.M. Ellwood for J.S. Henry. The screen panels are in leaded glass and copper. The chair is inlaid with pewter and has burnished copper panels. Music cabinet inlaid with pewter and green and yellow woods. It has spring doors and copper handles and lock plates. This and 150 from Modern British Domestic Architecture and Decoration, 1901.

Plate 152. Wardrobe and wash-stand exhibited at Glasgow Exhibition, 1901, by Wylie and Lochhead. Note tall gallery of wash-stand. From The Artist, Vol. 32. Almost certainly by George Logan.

A.E. TAYLOR

He also designed for Wylie and Lochhead. See the hexagonal table, Plate 153, which was exhibited at the Glasgow Exhibition 1901. *The Studio*, Volume 33, 1904 illustrates some of his work in "maple stained grey, decorated with inlaid opal and opalescent glass, brightwood and block tin, an inexpensive substitute for silver" and some drawing room furniture "in maple stained a rich violet to go on an apple green carpet." He is better known for his watercolours.

A. WICKHAM JARVIS

His furniture appeared in *The Studio* at least from 1896 and in 1898 when there was a chair with its front legs continued up well above the level of the arms. He was an architect and teacher at the Camberwell School of Art. His 'quaint' furniture for Conamur, Sandgate, is illustrated in *Building News,* Volume 84, 1903.

EDGAR WOOD

In 1895 he sent a chair to the Arts and Crafts Guild Exhibition, Manchester and in 1898 furniture in oak and sycamore decorated with inlays and coloured gesso. A settle and chest of drawers designed by him were executed by J.S.C. Cair and assistants and F.W. Jackson.

FRANK BRANGWYN 1867-1956

The versatile decorator, painter and designer of carpets, windows and furniture was designing furniture at least from 1900 when a bed decorated by him was illustrated in *The Studio*, Volume 19. Although primarily a painter/decorator, of whom it was said "his mission was to decorate something, to make something that would fulfil a special purpose of adornment and permanently beautify some chosen place", he was an inventive designer. He often specified cherry wood, as for the bed with sliding panels to form a cupboard at the head illustrated in MBDAD, 1901. Many of his pieces have painted or inlaid panels. Plate 154.

Plate 153. Handsomely inlaid hexagonal table exhibited at Glasgow Exhibition, 1901. Possibly by A.E. Taylor. From The Artist, *Vol. 32.*

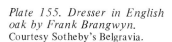

Plate 155. Dresser in English oak by Frank Brangwyn. Courtesy Sotheby's Belgravia.

Plate 154. Cabinet of cherry wood decorated with carved and coloured gesso by Frank Brangwyn and made by Paul Turpin, c.1910.
Courtesy Victoria and Albert Museum.

In 1909-10 he designed furniture for Casa Cuseni, Taormina.[14] He exhibited in Venice in 1905. His chair, table and carpet exhibited in Ghent in 1913 were executed by Turpin & Co. Plate 155 shows an original dresser by him.

In 1930 Pollard & Co. made and exhibited some exciting designs by him including earlier work and items in inlaid Circassian ash and oak and Indian grey wood inlaid with laurel. Some have art deco marquetry including an important art deco cabinet with side opening boxes on top.

JAMES HENRY SELLERS 1861-1954

Worked in or around Manchester. Architect and designer, not a craftsman and with Edgar Wood showed very expensive items in Arts and Crafts Society Exhibitions. He was still working c.1930. Plate 284. His designs often incorporated elaborate veneers.

EDWIN FOLEY

An angle cabinet by E.W. Foley was illustrated in the *Cabinet Maker,* Volume 6, p.193, in 1885. His designs, Plate 156, appeared in *The Artist* in 1898 and his ergonometric study, Plate 157, in January 1899. About 1910 he wrote the lavish *Book of Decorative Furniture. Its form, colour and history* (recently described as "authentic stockbroker belt literature").

WALTER EASSIE

Co-designer with Foley of Plate 156.

HARRY NAPPER

Designed some distinguished pieces for 'Officers' Ideal Quarters', made by Norman and Stacey and shown at the Earls Court Military Exhibition, 1901, Plates 158 and 159.

E.G. PUNNETT

According to W. Birch, grandson of the founder of the notable High Wycombe firm of William Birch, they made "quite a number of his models in wax finish, natural English walnut for Libertys."[15] His first design for them is thought to have been a rush seated arm chair, their No.906 (see Aslin and V and A), in 1901.

It was very similar to Plate 160. It is interesting that the only pages

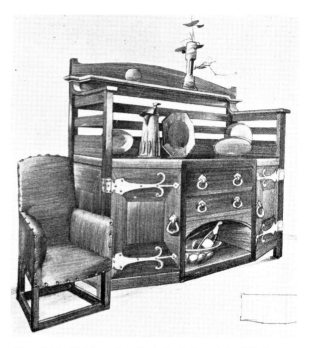

Plate 156. Sideboard and chair designed by Edwin Foley and Walter Eassie. From The Artist, *Vol. 23, 1898.*

Plate 157. Edwin Foley's diagram showing principles of comfort and discomfort in chair designing. The Artist, *Vol. 24, 1899.*

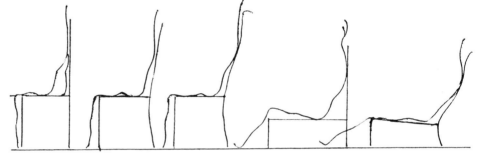

Plate 158. Double desk for ante-room in Officers' Mess designed by Harry Napper, and made by Norman and Stacey and exhibited at Earls Court Military Exhibition, 1901. From The Artist, *Vol. 31.*

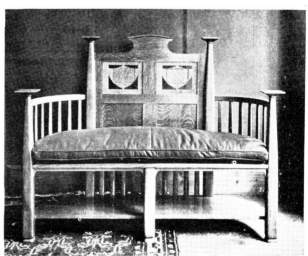

Plate 159. Hall settle in light oak designed by Harry Napper, made by Norman and Stacey and exhibited at Earls Court Military Exhibition, 1901. From The Artist, *Vol. 31.*

Plate 160. Chair very like that designed by Punnett for William Birch, possibly made by J. Pyment of the Guild of Handicrafts.

in Birch's Cost Books where Punnett's name appears are during October and November 1901 so perhaps he designed for them only briefly. But he made a considerable number of estimates and there is one note "Punnett cannot make again at this price" which suggests that perhaps he was a foreman or craftsman.

Plates 161 to 164 illustrate some Birch pieces which seem related to his known work, including their No.318A referred to as 'Punnett's Masterpiece'

C.R. ASHBEE 1863-1942, Architect

He was a very gifted designer of silver, a distinguished typographer and the founder, inspirer and administrator of the Guild of Handicrafts which had a showroom at 67a Bond Street (Dering Yard). In 1899 it was said "The bulk of the furniture design has fallen hitherto to Mr Ashbee"[16] but much of it was derivative, with, for example, elaborate writing desks based on varaguenos. He had a very able foreman craftsman in J.W. Pyment.

CHARLES SPOONER   ARIBA

In 1890 he exhibited a plain sideboard at the Arts and Crafts Exhibition. Some of his simple furniture, for example, a dresser with plank legs and long hinges, was illustrated in MBDAD, 1901. He worked with another architect craftsman Arthur Penty and together they founded Elmdon & Co., 1 Ravenscroft Park, Hammersmith, W. They held an exhibition at the Alpine Club in April 1905 and issued a catalogue price 2s. 6d. in July 1905. Most of the furniture was plain and Heal-like but they claimed that most of the designs were registered. They recommended customers to buy their mainly oak pieces unpolished and leave them to darken.

Plate 161, left. E.G. Punnett's name appears a score or so of times in a cost and design book of William Birch in October-November 1901. Among the items thus associated with him are those in Plates 161-164; whether he designed them all or only estimated for some is not clear.

Design 173a. Oak inlaid bureau with pierced plank legs. 'Mr. Punnett gave cost £8 19s.' 50in. x 30in.

Design 174a. Four foot square oak table extending to 8ft. by 4ft. Slip Punnett 15.10.1, earlier estimate 14.6.1.

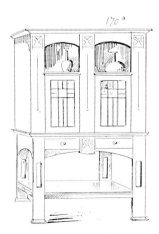

Plate 162. Birch No. 170a. Inlaid oak cabinet stained green, 17.5.1, polished £12 9s. Estimate for it in turned oak revised by Punnett 29.10.1. Still being made in 1906, then £9 15s.

Plate 163. Birch No. 185a. Wash-stand £3 3s. Dressing table £6 8s. 6d. Slip 18.11.1 Punnett.

Raised gallery round top of dressing table a feature of the time.

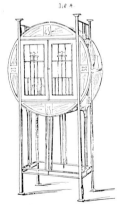

Plate 164. Birch No. 318A. Display cabinet 'Punnett's Masterpiece', £8 15s.

WILLIAM JAMES NEATBY

A designer of furniture, glass and metalwork. See MBDAD, 1901. He exhibited at Leeds Arts and Crafts Exhibition, 1901 a screen of peacock blue leather on green stained wood ornamented with blue and green enamels set in copper.

November 1901 Neatby and Evans advertised in *The Studio*.

R.S. LORIMER   ARSA, later Sir Robert, 1864-1929, Architect

See Plate 165.

MERVYN MACARTNEY, later Sir Mervyn, 1853-1932, Architect

See Plate 166.

L. WYBURD, A. DENNINGTON and E.P. ROBERTS

Designed for Liberty which was one of the most important firms making and selling high-quality progressive furniture.

HENRY TAYLOR WYSE

November 1899 he advertised in *The Studio* a Music and Print cabinet, price 65s. made by William Middleton, Arbroath. In 1900 he offered four large items all finished black, green or brown with copper mounts and coloured decorative panels. In 1901 there was a banner advertisement for his 'Simple Furniture' and an illustrated catalogue: "Simplicity of design, refinement of detail — beauty of colouring — honesty of workmanship — carriage paid to any railway station in Great Britain." The Scottish Guild of Handicrafts, Glasgow, his agent but no advertisements found after 1902. Several houses in Arbroath had furniture designed by him and made by W. Middleton.

A. ROMNEY GREEN 1872-1945

A brilliant mathematician who gave up teaching to become a craftsman. He had a workshop in Strand on the Green. He exhibited at Arts and Crafts Society Exhibitions at least from 1906. He continued to work into the 20s and 30s. See D. Joel's *The Adventure of British Furniture*.

ROGER FRY

He started the Omega Workshops in 1913. They produced a good deal of startlingly painted furniture but mainly after 1915. Plate 167.

CHARACTERISTICS OF PROGRESSIVE

Thus there were many strands in the field of progressive furniture from the mainly simple and traditional to the exciting, sophisticated work of Ellwood and Mackintosh and the gay, inventive pieces of Baillie Scott and others. There were new proportions and shapes. There were all kinds of inlay with enamels, glass, pewter and stained woods, whilst metalwork had become a very valuable decorative feature of many designs. Chair design and bedroom furniture in particular had developed. Plates 168-186 show additional examples.

To summarise, the following are specially characteristic features of the progessive:

— Punched out heart and spade shapes, and these in metalwork
— tulip shapes used as inlays, in textile design and in metalwork
— tall backs to chairs   *(continued p.123)*

Plate 165. Dresser by R.S. Lorimer, ARSA, in elm with inlaid hunting scene. From The British Home of Today, *1904.*

Plate 166. Cabinet of unpolished teak by Mervyn Macartney. From The British Home of Today, *1904.*

Plate 167. Painted chairs by Roger Fry's Omega Workshops. Grey with painted Omega sign, c.1913-14. Courtesy Sotheby's Belgravia.

Plate 168. Mahogany card table inlaid with fruitwood and mother-of-pearl briar rose panel, c.1900. Labelled Liberty.
Courtesy Sotheby's Belgravia.

Plate 169. Chair after a Baillie Scott design for Darmstadt. Hide seat missing.

Plate 170. Early twentieth century chair with characteristic inlay, tall back and triple stretchers.
Courtesy Sotheby's Belgravia.

Plate 171. Upholstered chair with tall sides and original upholstery, stamped T.S.G. The tall tapering supports are cross banded in satinwood, c.1900.
Courtesy Sotheby's Belgravia.

Plate 172. Chair inlaid with woods and mother-of-pearl. In early twentieth century catalogue of Wylie and Lochhead as No. 668, price 48s. 6d.

Plate 173. A mahogany and fruitwood settle, the top rail inlaid with stylised tulips, c.1900.
Courtesy Sotheby's Belgravia.

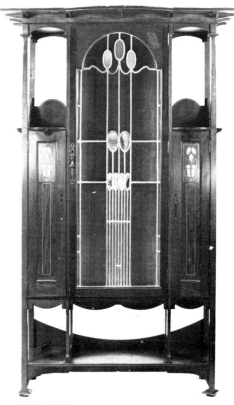

Plate 174. Mahogany cabinet numbered R. 2033, the doors with stained glass oval panels, the side doors with mother-of-pearl and fruitwood stylised floral panels, c.1900.
Courtesy Sotheby's Belgravia.

Plate 175. Mahogany and marquetry side cabinet with fall front, inlaid with beechwood clematis and metal hearts. It has the sinuous lines characteristic of art nouveau work.
Courtesy Sotheby's Belgravia.

— floor level and triple stretchers
— overhanging cornices and shelves and mushroom finials
— tall supports sometimes composed of four separate shafts, sometimes simple pillars
— sinuous shapes often incorporating the whiplash motif
— sloping sides of sideboards, chests and canted table legs
— projecting central sections of sideboards with cut back sides
— copper hinges and pewter inlay
— raised galleries and flat cap toppings
— plank legs and broad flat arms
— some wood left untreated, some oiled or waxed, some stained a colour

But already by 1899 *The House Beautiful*, published in Chicago, had sensed that continental designers were advancing more inventively and progressively and pronounced "England, the mother of the modern decorative movement, now seems likely to give up the leadership she has so firmly held for twenty years."

Plate 176. Single chair on left made by William Birch. Note mushroom finials. Rocking chair with inlaid splat. Both c.1900.
Courtesy Mrs. K.H. Bulcock

Some time fairly soon after 1905 or 1906 a new mood can be detected in magazine articles and advertisements. Much reproduction work was available; and the craze for collecting antiques, unfortunately, fostered backward looking sentiments. There was a new Queen Anne revival, this time including cabriole legged chairs, and, gradually, even progressive firms like J.S. Henry, Libertys and Heals are found advertising reproductions even in *The Studio*. In 1904 Heals offered 'Reproductions of Early Georgian Bedroom Furniture' and in 1908 a Queen Anne bed, whilst J.S. Henry asserted 'Reproductions of Antique Furniture a speciality'. In 1907 Wylie and Lochhead showed traditional mahogany and in 1909 a Jacobean flavoured advertisement, whilst Heals offered 'colonial Adam' and Libertys a catalogue 'Reproductions of 17th century Furniture'.

Since the winter of 1903 there had been increasing references to economic distress in the trade.[17] The challenge from cut price imports had grown and by 1910 trade conditions were distinctly difficult; even Waring and Gillows were in trouble and their long delayed accounts regarded as far from satisfactory.

Thus in the first decade of the twentieth century, when the progressive should have been blossoming forth on to a market well prepared for it, trade itself was so precarious that even makers who wanted to offer the new work had to proceed very cautiously. Unfortunately, the trade was all too controlled by the often ill educated, small minded buyers of the retail stores. Schooled in the traditional, few of them had the eyes or imagination to see the good in the new and so manufacturers, already hard pressed, had to protect themselves by providing yet more of the repro which the trade buyers

Ethelbert

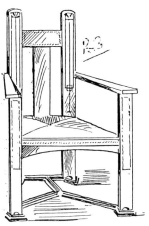

Plate 177, left. William Birch No. 871, 'The Ethelbert', 40s. polished, in 1901. This sturdy chair was advertised in Liberty's Yuletide Catalogue in 1899 at £3 7s. 6d.

Plate 178. William Birch No. 920, page dated 16.9.1901, 'oak rush arm' 65s. 6d. Floor level stretchers popular then.

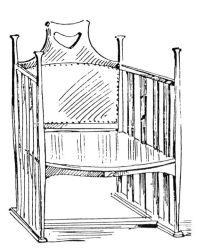

Plate 179. William Birch No. 944, Liberty No. 5 arm chair in the white £1 7s. 3d., solid rosewood 54s. 6d., in 1901.

Plate 180. William Birch No. 155a, inlaid mahogany cabinet 16.9.1901, stock size 72 by 42in., £10 10s. Plank legs and cut away angled fronts fashionable then.

were prepared to order. There is a very revealing report in the *Cabinet Maker* of October 1903 in which a Mr Ingram of the firm of Mason and Watkinson of Durban considered the New Art needed a little fostering but would ultimately make a success. But other South African buyers "thought that at any rate for the present, the older styles were better adhered to." These sentiments must have been echoed by many firms' buyers.

So that just when this 'New Art', the progressive, could offer exciting possibilities with well made, rather unusual furniture decorated with imaginative metal mounts and bold inlay, trade was so precarious that most makers could not take the risk for long and had to fall back on the safer, staid repro.

The Studio Year Book of 1911 reported in its section on Decorative and Applied Art in Great Britain: "In surveying the work which has been produced during the last few years one cannot fail to be impressed by the prevailing lack of originality in design. The few attempts made to break away from accepted models have in most cases ended in failure while in nearly all directions we find nothing but reproductions of the old styles. This death of ideas applies more especially to furniture/...

"If we inquire into the cause of this stagnant condition we are told that the public is responsible for it, that the popular demand for copies of the antique has compelled the manufacturer to confine his productions to the hackneyed models. We are not prepared, however, to accept this as the only explanation. May it not be that the public is compelled to accept these reproductions, because it is almost impossible to obtain any good original designs? . . ." It continued:

Plate 181. William Birch No. 269a, inlaid mahogany whatnot £1 8s. 6d., in oak 24s.

Plate 182. William Birch No. 603 referred to as 'antique oak-arm.' Another version No. 604, has legs continuing up to support arms 21.10.00. Similar to a design by George Walton.

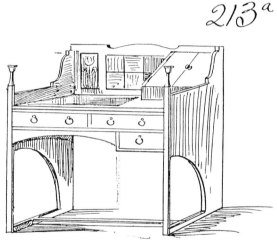

Plate 184, left. William Birch No. 213a, inlaid mahogany writing table 9.5.2., £6 10s. each, plus lining when made two at a time.
Note upright projections and solid ends. 41 by 39 inches.

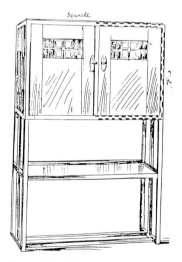

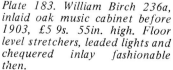

Plate 185, left. William Birch No. 929, inlaid oak settee stained blue green or fumed oak, frame £6 10s. in 16.9.01.

Plate 183. William Birch 236a, inlaid oak music cabinet before 1903, £5 9s. 55in. high. Floor level stretchers, leaded lights and chequered inlay fashionable then.

Footnotes

1. From a sheet bound into the back of 1887 volume of The Century Guild Work and noted in the Handley Read files.
2. *The Artist*, Vol. 24, p.14, January 1899.
3. Benson included one of this shape in his *Elements of Handicraft Design*, 1893.
4. *Cabinet Maker*, Vol. 8, July 1887.
5. *The Builder*, Vol. 59, p.285, October 11, 1890.
6. *The Artist*, Vol. 24, p.14, January 1899.
7. From notes in the Handley Read files in the RIBA archives.
8. Details from M. Burroughs *Connoisseur*, CLXXI and CLXXII, 1969.
9. *Cabinet Maker*, Vol. 9, p.141, December 1888.
10. *Building News*, Vol. 71, p.845, December 11, 1896.
11. *The Studio*, Vol. 42, October 1907.
12. *The Studio*, Vol. 32, p.240, August 1904.
13. *The Artist*, Vol. 23, p.147, 1898.
14. Details and photographs in Handley Read files in RIBA archives.
15. Letter 8.1.60 from William Birch to Elizabeth Aslin in a Birch cost book in High Wycombe Reference Library.
16. *The Studio*, Vol. 18, p.104, November 1899.
17. *Cabinet Maker*, November 1903.

"The Arts and Crafts movement which gave promise of such great things has almost ceased to exist, and the interest aroused by its advent has not been sustained because so much of the recent work has given small cause for enthusiasm. The result has been that the public has been compelled to return to the old models."

It must have been a very depressing time. Mackmurdo had already retired to the country in 1901 — to Essex to study economics. The firm of J.P. White which had made Baillie Scott's furniture ceased to advertise it after 1905 and soon retreated to their old line in garden furniture. Mackintosh lost heart after 1909 and in 1914 retired to Suffolk to paint and drink and even Baillie Scott went to live abroad in 1913. Few of the designers listed above are heard of in the period 1910-15 except Ambrose Heal and the Cotswolders, and presumably more than a few of them were killed in the slaughter of 1914-18.

A generation which could produce the drama of Mackintosh, the elegant work of Walton, the appealing pieces of Baillie Scott and the sophistication of Ellwood should have had a rich harvest. But, having developed over a quarter of a century, the progressive was then cut off before it had fully arrived and before its rich and varied possibilities had been fully explored and exploited.

The Cotswolders and some other craftsmen carried on producing finely proportioned work of high quality but the dynamism had gone. For this a new generation was needed.

Plate 186. Brass bedstead, c.1900.

CHAPTER 6

Woods,Finishes and some Fashions and Innovations

WOODS AND FINISHES

Many items especially bedroom suites were offered in a selection of woods and finishes. Ranging in order of cost from the cheapest these were: deal, japanned any colour, enamelled, solid ash, American walnut, solid mahogany, rosewood. Many items, especially tables, chairs, sideboards and bookcases were offered in oak, walnut and mahogany at the same price.

Pine and other softwoods were much used for bedroom furniture, sometimes French polished until "the grain of it shows much of the delicacy and agreeableness of satinwood."

Oak: much of the oak used was Baltic oak known as 'wainscott'. This was cheaper than English oak and American was cheaper still. A great deal of oak was darkened by being fumed with ammonia; some was simply oiled or waxed and some treated with a 'dead' polish.

Teak cost fifteen per cent more than English oak in 1905 and was not much used.

Satinwood was favoured for bedrooms and drawing rooms in the Louis Seize manner.

Mahogany varied from handsomely grained woods of high quality to an unattractive black variety later. It was usually given a high gloss with French polish but some was fumed and some ebonized.

American Walnut was used a great deal; English walnut less as it was more expensive.

Rosewood became more popular again in the 80s and Lucrafts were commended in 1886 for "Being first in the field with the new and delightful combination of rosewood and chased ivory."

Basswood (American lime) which is yellow at first but turns, via a dirty mustard colour, to grey brown, was being used from about 1880.

Jarrah, an Australian wood, rather like a pinkish mahogany was available from the mid 80s and was recommended to contrast well with ebony and American walnut.

Colours: Dull black and ebonized finishes were especially popular in the 1870s and 80s even for Windsor chairs. Green staining was popular in the 80s and into the late 90s. It continued to be popular for bedroom furniture into the early years of this century when "blue, terracotta, red

Plate 187. Inlaid mahogany bureau bookcase, 2ft. 7in. wide, 6ft. 5in. high, c.1910. An example of good quality 'Edwardian' style. Courtesy Sotheby's Belgravia.

Plate 188. *Wardrobe, in the 'architectural Queen Anne' manner, designed by John Small and made by Chapman & Son, Newcastle and North Shields, c.1882.*

Plate 189. *Design for a 'Beaconsfield' wardrobe by W. Timms. This asymmetrical, multi-purpose type popular from the mid-1880s.* Cabinet Maker, *February 1886.*

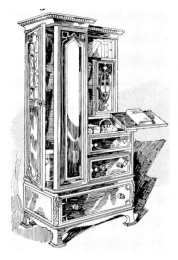

Plate 190. *This multi-purpose wardrobe, designed by H. Pringuer, appeared in the* Cabinet Maker *in February 1899. Note reading slide.*

and even crimson" also were fashionable. "Paint and enamel not only in white and cream, but in various other tints"[1] also were in vogue for bedroom furniture throughout this period.

Inlay was an important form of decoration: in elaborate tarsia or certosino work, in various woods for floral marquetry on Victorian style pieces, in bone on Edwardian style items and in pewter, enamel, glass, mother-of-pearl and stained woods on progressive work. Dark and light checked stringing was one of the hallmarks of turn of the century pieces.

THE EDWARDIAN STYLE

This is a style which could not be classified in the previous chapter as progressive but, rather, needs to be considered separately. Out of all the designs more and less in later eighteenth century styles came a recognisably 'Edwardian' style. It had digested features from Chippendale, Adam, Hepplewhite and Sheraton but it mixed them in new ways, on new shapes and with different proportions, usually in mahogany but often in satinwood and frequently inlaid with bone. Much of it is of fine craftsmanship, as in Plate 187; but much of it is too lightweight as the keen price competition of that time caused many makers to use wood very sparingly. It is seat furniture in particular that appears too insubstantial with legs distinctly too slender. But plenty of this Edwardian style is available, so buyers can afford to be selective.

The rest of this chapter cannot be all embracing; it aims merely to bring together strands of information about items which varied widely or, for some reason, were specially notable in this period.

BEDROOM FURNITURE

There was the greatest variety from the highly or moderately elaborate (Plate 191) to the rather refined suites as in Plates 88 and 90, to the downright plain (Plate 192); and from the fussy 'quaint' (Plate 194) to the spare, elegant progressive. Plates 124 and 134.

WARDROBES

Loudon had regretted in 1833 that "chests of drawers are the common substitute for wardrobes"[2] and despite the disadvantages of drawer and tray storage, this must have continued to be the custom for nearly half a century as in 1889 the Booth survey noted "A change of fashion that deserves mention for the considerable effect it has had on the trade is the extensive substitution of wardrobes for chests of drawers."[3] Certainly wardrobes became important items in this period. In expensive bedroom suites it was said, in 1892, the previous "utilitarian and rigidly severe simplicity of character was replaced by costly magnificence of design ... the modern wardrobe being not only a receptacle for clothes but also a thing of ornamental interest."[4] As "the customer who can spend 100 guineas or more on a bedroom suite very naturally desires to avoid patronising a transient style", Queen Anne or Louis Seize were recommended.

In less expensive suites, one of the most welcome changes noted the *Cabinet Maker* in February 1886, was "the breaking up of the Wardrobe. Then the lines were formal and the parts equally divided, now the lopsided but useful Beaconsfield (Plate 189) has become one of the most popular robes on the market." Such multi-purpose wardrobes had book and display shelves in addition to drawers and cupboards. The ends sometimes had open shelves and fret cut decoration. The wardrobe in Plate 190 by the hack designer Pringuer even provided a book slope so that its owner could read his daily portion of whatever whilst struggling with his collar stud. In 1887 Marsh Jones and Cribb exhibited at the Saltaire Golden Jubilee Show a wardrobe "in the fashionable fumed mahogany and original in that it had no long glass door". Maurice B. Adam's design, Plate 88, also was without one.

Fitted wardrobes gradually found favour after Robert Edis' recommendation of fitted bedrooms in the mid 80s (Plate 91). Another innovation was the production of corner wardrobes designed to make the best use of space in small rooms. An oddity was the 'Benedict' bedroom suite (1885) with 'his' and 'hers' duplicated items. The wardrobe had two cupboards and two mirrors to prevent 'the agitation of marital tempers'.

Plate 191. 'Italian Renaissance' dressing table with its arched glass and niches recommended to be made in rosewood and ivory, Cabinet Maker, *July 1, 1886.*

Plate 192. This 'Desideratum' gentleman's dressing room suite registered by J.C. Mineard and Co., Barnsbury Grove, north London. Cabinet Maker, *February 1882.*

Plate 193. Oak chest of drawers with raised gallery and incised geometrical pattern. The little brackets and decoration suggest the influence of Christopher Dresser. Locks stamped R.L. and Co. 1880s?
Courtesy Sotheby's Belgravia.

Plate 194. *Bedroom suite, considered distinctly new by* Cabinet Maker, *July 1892.*

Plate 195. Liberty wash-stand probably designed by Leonard R. Wyburd. The frieze is inlaid with pewter tulip heads. The printed canvas back is secured with leather thongs. It has lattice sides and the top covered with pewter sheet. The doors have a wooden rod lock. 63 by 35in., c.1900.

DRESSING TABLES AND CHESTS

For the richer customer wanting a non transient style, makers were recommended in 1886 "to couple the cultured spirit of the Renaissance with our more quaint and patriotic 'Queen Anne' or with the elegant and graceful Louis Seize".[5] Of Plate 43, it was said: "The little pediments on the top of the glass, the shaped pieces at the sides and the quaint details in the doors are appropriate in feeling to the Victorian Queen Anne sort of architecture which is now so much in vogue." [6] Rosewood and ivory were recommended for the 'Italian Renaissance' design in Plate 191.

Far more restrained forms were offered by Maurice B. Adams in his designs for Gillows and Robertsons in Plates 88 and 90. Of Plate 90 he said "economy has been considered coupled with an endeavour to give interest to the general design of things primarily intended to be useful and clean in wear."[7]

Original Design for a Simple Bedroom Suite,
by Mr. E. Pite.

Plate 196. "Original Design for a Simple Bedroom Suite by Mr. E. Pite." Edis would have disapproved of this. Cabinet Maker, April 1899.

Plate 197, right. Inlaid oak wax polished wash-stand and dressing table No. 198a. William Birch design book, c.1900. Note overhangs, ring handles and upward projections. Trade prices £5 9s. 6d. and £7 2s. 6d.

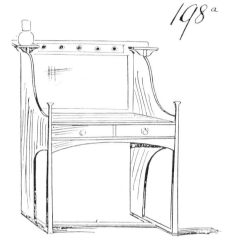

198ª

Plate 192 shows a severely plain dressing chest 'The Desideratum' which must have seemed very advanced when its design was registered in 1882.

The unusual 'Benedict' was supplied with two mirrors because "Where is the married man who has not, in the case of the usual single mirror toilet table been compelled to wait for his wife to finish her back hair before he could proceed . . .?"

Progressive and quaint dressing tables often had inward sloping sides and overhanging tops with pointed ends. Plate 194. In the 90s they were often stained green.

WASH-STANDS

Wash-stands of course shared the decorative characteristics of dressing tables. The 'Benedict', inevitably, had space for two jugs and basins. That in Plate 194 was considered in 1892 to show "a decided freshness of thought in the style, formation and general character." The Liberty wash-stand, Plate 195, probably by L. Wyburd c.1898 also has the popular canted sides which had been featured by W.A.S. Benson in 1884. Plate 106.

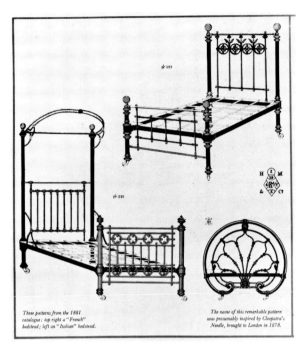

Plate 198. *Registered designs for metal beds from the 1881 catalogue of Horatio Myers reproduced in* Myer's First Century 1876-1976. *Top right a 'French' bedstead, left an 'Italian.'*

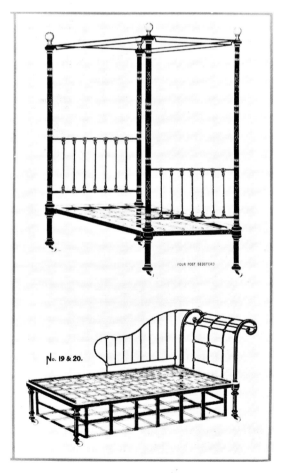

The innovation in wash-stand design was the addition of towel rails. Did E.W. Godwin first introduce it in his Bedroom Furniture, Plate 72, before 1877? It does not appear to have caught on quickly as it was not until 1891 that Pringuer mentioned "The towel rail as a separate institution has almost become a thing of the past . . . its incorporation with the wash-stand is certainly a happy idea."[8] But Gillows and many other firms were still supplying them with elaborate suites up to the end of this period.

PROGRESSIVE BEDROOM SUITES

It was for bedroom furniture that the progressive style had the longest run. Gillows, Wylie and Lochhead and Heals were still advertising them around 1910. Gillows had made some attractive suites with punched through hearts, stencilled art nouveau designs and leaded lights for the Midland Hotel, Manchester.

BEDS

At the beginning of this period metal beds mainly made in Birmingham had long been popular. Plates 198 and 199 show new designs by the recently founded London firm of Horatio Myers. But Gillows exhibit of a wooden bed at the Fine Art and Industries Exhibition in Manchester in 1882 was hailed as a welcome protest against the metallic fashion and led to a vogue for wooden beds. Beds with high wings as in Plates 200 and 258 were popular around 1900 as were twin beds.

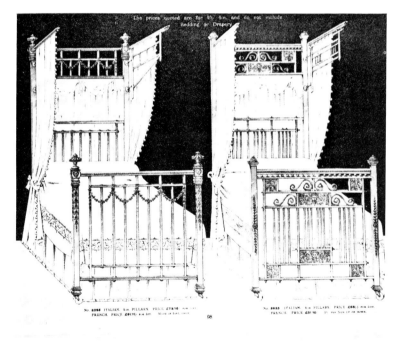

Plate 200, above. *Brass 'Italian' metal beds with high wings by Horatio Myers. Left with "Italian 2in. pillars £73 10s. French £61 11s." Right "Italian 2in. pillars £63, French £51 10s." A pre-1914 catalogue.*

Plate 199, left. *Extending bed and cheap popular four poster by Horatio Myers, also from 1881 catalogue.*

DINING ROOM FURNITURE

The forthright Mrs. Loftie in her book *The Dining Room,* 1878, in the 'Art in the Home' series, having wondered "... If builders and architects ever allowed the idea to cross their minds that houses were places to live in ...", put forward sound ideas as to the dining room's appearance: "Indeed where the dining room is used for breakfast it ought to be particularly cheerful. It is the place where the family meet first in the morning to take their tone for the day. The children are going to their lessons and want to be brightened up. The master of the house is reading his business letters and must be kept in good temper. The mother has perhaps before her a tiring, laborious day and requires cheering to carry her hopefully through her work."!

The dining room in middle class homes doubled as an extra living room and it was generally agreed that it should be in masculine taste. In addition to its dining table and chairs, sideboard and possibly dinner waggon and cabinet it required a nine piece suite consisting of lady's chair, gentleman's chair, couch and six single chairs. All were to be upholstered preferably in leather and otherwise in imitation leather or 'saddle bags' or Utrecht velvet. Roan leather seems to have been about two thirds the price of Morocco. Very often the rectangular wooden framework of these chairs was hidden by the upholstery and the padded arms supported by rows of spindles.

DINING CHAIRS

There was the greatest variety. The most fashionable 'modern' and unattractive chair in the 80s and 90s had a rectangular framed upholstered back panel joined to the top rail and uprights by turned spindles. Legs were usually turned and decorated with incised rings but some were square. Plates 201 and 203 show good examples of progressive dining chairs.

DINING TABLES

There were few developments in tables. The 'telescopic', that is the rectangular table made to take additional leaves and often with rounded ends, continued to be popular. The stout turned legs often had incised rings and low relief carving.

There were expanding circular tables with wooden segments of a larger circle appearing from beneath and running in grooves.

SIDEBOARDS

Sideboards in this period were sometimes known simply as 'boards'. Like wardrobes, they became in most styles, more complex with extra shelves and drawers. Many progressive sideboards had sloping sides, important long hinges and metal mounts and sometimes carved or painted mottoes or quotations as in Chapter 5.

DRAWING ROOM FURNITURE

By 1880 there had recently been a dramatic change in the accepted mode of furnishing drawing rooms. Whereas of the fashionable drawing

Plate 201. Oak single chair from a set of eight dining chairs, arched back inlaid with pewter and ebony, characteristic tapering legs and shaped feet, c.1900. Courtesy Sotheby's Belgravia.

Plate 202. Oak carver from a set of dining chairs registered by Joseph Johnstone, Loch Winnoch, 1912; 'new look' old ladder-back.

Plate 203. Oak dining chair with shaped and curved splat, c.1900. Note cut out heart shapes. Similar chairs have been found labelled Goodyer, Regent Street.

Plate 204. Liberty 'Hathaway' oak dresser in catalogue, c.1905-10. Characteristic overhang, feet, 'bottle' glass and projecting angled centre section.

room of c.1870 it was said "The only style of furnishing the drawing room was: couch or settee on one side and the chiffonier facing the eagle crowned mirror on the other and a glossy loo oval table in the centre; lady's and gentleman's chairs on either side of the fireplace and six small upright chairs arranged demurely round the remaining wall space. Such a stiff disposition of the leading reception room was eventually broken up by some and the fashion came into vogue of filling this apartment with any oddments that had pretence to beauty or comfort. When once the fixed law of having a 'Set Suite' was transgressed by the leaders of fashion, admission into the drawing room was obtained for a crowd of chairs of all names, shapes and sizes."[9]

So it was that the last quarter of the nineteenth century came to produce a far greater variety of chairs than any other.

CHAIRS

Low upholstered chairs were known as 'gossips'. There were other 'occasionals', tête-à-têtes, fancy rush seated chairs, the one time kitchen Windsor now "risen to the dignity of a patrician" and many spindly 'fancy' chairs (Plates 206-216). There were still, of course, the deeply upholstered ottomans, Chesterfields and club easy chairs which, since the 1860s, had been made so extra comfortable by the addition of a top stuffing of cotton and cotton wool combings over the springs. This permitted even deeper and more opulent looking buttoning. Velvets, silks and some tapestries were favoured for drawing room upholstery. In the increasingly health conscious 80s, the realisation of the probable danger from dust and germs in upholstery, encouraged many to favour loose cushions and led to many chairs being made with an opening between the seat and the upholstery of the back.

There were too the many tall backed progressive and 'quaint' chairs (Plates 114 and 138), spring rockers like the 'Restawell', folding chairs, Parker's adjustable spring easy chair, the fore-runner of the 'Recliner' from 1891 and a host of others including wicker, bamboo (Plate 250) and all the Austrian bentwood varieties. Plate 216.

In November 1892 the *Cabinet Maker* remarked "When once the old suite of nine traditions were broken through, there rushed into the drawing room an army of these spider like chairs.

". . . One can but rejoice in the rich variety of pattern and general excellence of the workmanship which is found in many of these somewhat fragile goods. If some complain that they are too fragile we can only take comfort in the thought 'So much better for the trade'."

OCCASIONAL TABLES

Some of the newer types were "the modern octagonal tea tables with nether balconies and plateaus", the Godwin type coffee table (Plate 72), the round or polygonal topped table with slim tapering legs (Plate 217), the spread leg tables and those with pierced plank legs (Plates 219 and 220). Some articles refer to 'five o'clock tea tables' but the *Furniture Trade Catalogue* of 1882 refers only to coffee tables not tea.

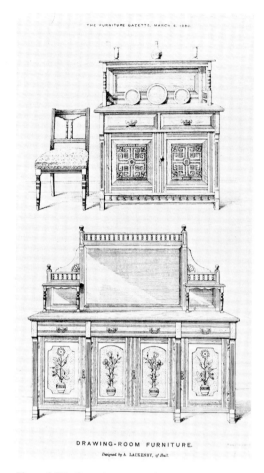

Plate 205. Drawing room furniture designed by A. Lackenby of Hull, published in Furniture Gazette, *March 6, 1880, with the spindles, incised lines, painted panels and Japanese fret pattern characteristic of art furniture.*

Plate 206. This cane seated chair supplied by Morris and Co. to Standen, East Grinstead, c.1890 is almost an exact copy of one which lies in the foreground of C.R. Leslie's 'Londoner's Gypsying', painted c.1820, illustrated Furniture History, *1972.* Courtesy Mrs. P.M. Wager.

Plate 207. This small cane seated folding chair appears as No. 280 in 1870/80 catalogue of William Collins and Son, Downley, High Wycombe.

Plate 208. A finely crafted example which appeared in a catalogue of Benjamin North 1860s/70s and in one of C. and R. Light, 1881.

Plate 209. 'The Saville' armchair thought to have been designed for Morris and Co. by George Jack, c.1890. It originally retailed at £7 5s.
Courtesy Sotheby's Belgravia.

Plate 210. Stained and inlaid chair in beech, High Wycombe, 1890s.

Plate 211. Stained beech chair with crossed stretchers, seat in alternate natural and red stained rushes, last quarter of the nineteenth century.

Plate 212. 'The Argylle' appears in Liberty's 'Dining Room and Library Furniture' catalogue 1890s?: "Strong and artistic, rush seated in oak, mahogany or walnut or blackwood, in black 19s. 6d." Settee, lady's and gentleman's and six single chairs only 10 guineas.

Plate 213. Popular early twentieth century rush seated arm chair in oak made by William Birch, No. 3014a, 13s. 6d. in 1907. In Wolfe and Hollander catalogue at 30s., early twentieth century.

Plate 214, left. 'The Tenaty' by Goodearl Brothers in Cabinet Maker, January 1905.

Plate 216, right. Bentwood nursing chair, labelled and stamped Thonet.

Plate 215. Stained beech arm chair with splat and high back characteristic of around 1900. Stamped 'C.V.' S.

Plate 217, left. Octagonal rosewood centre table with moulded edge and eight slender legs joined by arcaded apron with eight stretchers radiating from a central column. A table like this has been seen stamped: Collinson and Lock. c.1880.
Courtesy Sotheby's Belgravia.

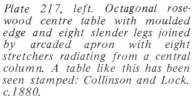

Plate 218, above. Octagonal oak table, turned legs decorated with ebony pegs, c.1880. Courtesy Victoria and Albert Museum.

Plate 219. Oak table with shaped top and each angled leg incised with long stemmed tulip, c.1900.

Plate 220. Circular inlaid mahogany occasional table, 'No. 200 new design Price £2 9s. 6d.' in Norman and Stacey Ltd. ('under Royal Patronage') catalogue, c.1910. This, with shaped and cut through inward facing plank legs was designed by G.M. Ellwood for J.S. Henry, c.1900.

CABINETS

In 1892 the *Cabinet Maker* noted "the cabinet of any arrangement of shelves, drawers and cupboards has replaced the stern chiffonier." Curvaceous low examples as in Plate 5 were still being made but the new fashionable cabinet was taller, Plate 223. Plate 221 shows an ebonized art movement example. Plate 224 illustrates later progressive inlaid cabinets. The firm of Morris and Co. specialised in very elaborate inlaid and/or painted cabinets. Plate 141.

Hanging cabinets and open shelves were popular in the 80s and 90s. A drawing room needed one large and two or three small display cabinets to house the harvest of 'chinamania'. Corner cabinets were popular for this purpose.

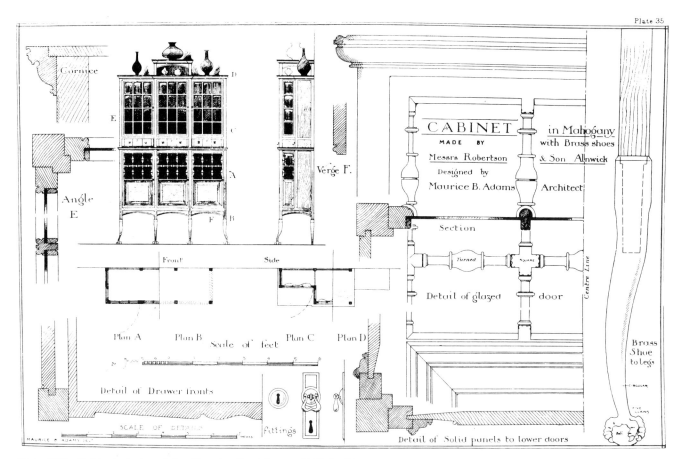

Plate 223. Cabinet designed by Maurice B. Adams, FRIBA. Made in mahogany with brass shoes by Robertson and Son, Alnwick. ". . . Designed for inexpensive manufacture, the doors being repeats of each other." Shown at Manchester Exhibition, 1886.

Plate 221. Art movement ebonized cabinet with characteristic spindles, painted panels, bevelled mirrors, brackets and gilt incised lines. Stamped Edwards and Roberts 1870s/80s.
Courtesy Sotheby's Belgravia.

Plate 222. Cabinet designed by John Small for John Pollock of Beith: "Designed after Chippendale and Sheraton and has been principally made in dark mahogany, though occasionally in walnut. The plain panels are made of richly figured wood while the other parts are of a uniformly straight grain ... successfully sold amongst the trade," c.1881.

Plate 224. Mahogany cabinet labelled 'Christopher Pratt and Sons, Cabinet Maker and Upholsterer, Bradford,' and numbered 17340. Inlaid with mother-of-pearl and fruitwood tulips and foliage, heart shaped top panel has intertwined tulip, pewter glazing bars, 76 by 54in. Early twentieth century.

CORNER FITMENTS

'Cosy corners' were a popular feature of the 90s. "The latest demand of fashionable caprice being a demand for corner furnishings" it was said in May, 1892 and Flora Thompson, in *Lark Rise to Candleford*, mentions "cosy corners... built of old boxes and covered with cretonne."

INGLE-NOOKS

These too were popular in the 90s as in Plate 227 and as in progressive designs like that of Ellwood's in Plate 147.

SCREENS

"Screens of late years have had a new lease of life displaying fabrics, glass, marqueterie, carving and painting."[10] The firm of H. & J. Cooper invented the little screen with a teacup shelf, and more important, they introduced the divisional spindle screen, c.1882, which may have influenced Mackmurdo and have promoted the idea of the cosy corner. There were too, little 'window screens' to place on tables, presumably, to ensure privacy. Plate 228 shows a combination of screen and seats.

Plate 226. Whatnot by Morris and Co. with "... long spindles and fretwork gallery as the common vogue but very well done" noted Cabinet Maker, Vol. 4, p.141, 1884.

Plate 225. Cabinet inscribed 'Robson and Sons, 47 Northumberland St., Newcastle-on-Tyne.' Inlaid with tulips, sinuous foliage and 'whip-lash' roots, c.1900.
Courtesy Sotheby's Belgravia.

BOOKCASES

There were revolving bookcases earlier in the century but they were not common before the rectangular revolving types as in Plate 229 in the 1890s.

Globe Wernicke, the 'elastic' bookcase, 'always complete but never finished' sectional bookcases were available from 1884. Minty followed and William Baker advertised the 'Oxford Sectional Bookcase' from 1911.

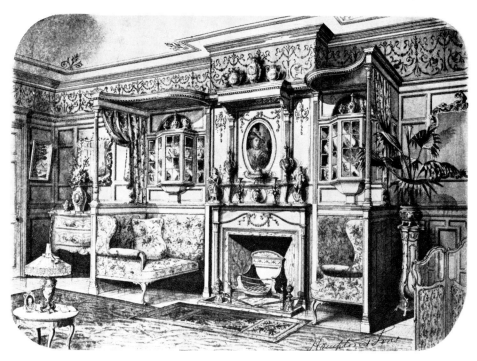

Plate 227. Ingle-nooks were popular in traditional rooms as here as well as in progressive schemes in the 1890s. Catalogue of Hampton and Sons, c.1900.

Plate 228. Combination screen with shelves and settee. Cabinet Maker, *July 1897.*

Plate 229. New 'Times' Encyclopaedia Revolving Bookcase and Reading Stand. Design registered by Matthews & Co. Cabinet Maker, *April 1899.*

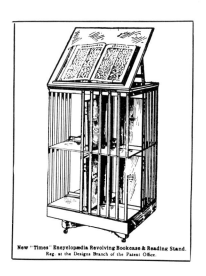

141

Plate 230. The popular roll
top desk and rotary chairs
by William Angus and Co.
and many makers, c.1900.

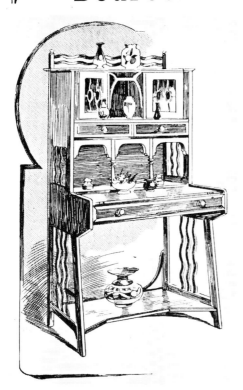

Plate 231, left.
Writing desk by
Maples with the
then popular wavy
lath decoration.
Cabinet Maker,
January 1899.

Plate 232. Ebonized writing desk of type
popular around 1900. Has characteristic long
copper hinges and overhanging top. The
other contemporary items reflect the current
obsession with elongation. The chair has its
original 'tulip' seating fabric.

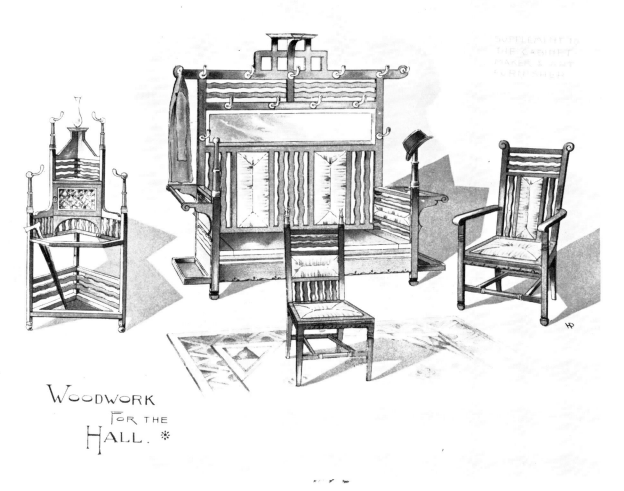

Plate 233. 'Woodwork for the Hall'. This design was the first coloured sheet issued by a furniture journal in the United Kingdom. The items were stained in the then popular green. Cabinet Maker, *July 1895.*

Plate 234. An improved safer model of Lawes and Co.'s 'Child's Table Chair' which converted to the 'Eclipse Spring Phaeton.' Cabinet Maker, 1880.

Plate 235. Bachelor's Settle designed by Edwin Foley, a multi-purpose piece ranging from thermometer holder to coal scuttle. The Artist, *Vol. 23, 1898.*

DESKS

Roll top varieties were the most popular desks in this period with many imported from the U.S. and Canada. Pratts of Bradford produced a small one Reg. No. 380081 from 1901. Slim types as in Plates 231 and 232 were popular c.1895-1910.

HALL FURNITURE

It was very varied but the simple forms suited to hall furniture looked well in the progressive manner. Attractive examples appear in Wylie and Lochhead's catalogues around 1900. Plate 233 was the first to appear in colour in a furniture journal in 1895.

MULTI-PURPOSE

Some items, e.g. wardrobes with drawers, cupboards, book and display shelves, came to be designed for the many smaller houses and flats. Plate 235.

Footnotes

1. Guy Bentley in Alison Adburgham's *Liberty's, a biography of a shop,* 1975.
2. Loudon's *Encyclopaedia of Cottage, Farm and Villa Architecture and Furniture,* 1833.
3. Charles Booth, *Life and Labour of the People of London,* Vol. 4; The Trades of East London . . . in the year 1888. Chapter 6. Ernest Aves: The Furniture Trade.
4. *Cabinet Maker,* p.215, February 1892.
5. *Cabinet Maker,* Vol. 7, p.9, July 1, 1886.
6. ibid, p.10.
7. Maurice B. Adams, *Examples of old English houses and furniture drawn by MBA, architect, with some modern works from designs by the author,* 1888.
8. *Cabinet Maker,* Vol. 12, p.63, September 1891.
9. *Cabinet Maker,* Vol. 1, p.85, December 1880.
10. *Cabinet Maker,* Vol. 13, p.115, November 1892.

CHAPTER 7

Exact Copies and Fakes

Plate 236. This chair labelled Wright and Mansfield shows the high quality of their reproduction work, probably 1880s.
Courtesy Victoria and Albert Museum.

What constitutes a fake?

Some fakes are made; some items have the role thrust upon them.

An exact copy may be an honest reproduction and sold as such but if it is later sold with intent to deceive, the same item becomes a fake. Many so-called seventeenth and eighteenth century pieces began life in the late nineteenth century as high quality reproductions and as these are, and will be, on the market it is useful to be aware of the extent and quality of the reproduction trade then.

High quality copies were made from the 1870s to 1886 by Wright and Mansfield. Plate 236. They specialised in Chippendale, Hepplewhite, Sheraton and Louis Seize and often labelled their work.

Edwards and Roberts of Wardour Street also affixed labels and so skilful was much of their work that when these labelled pieces are studied it is not always apparent whether the labels denote production by them or merely repairs. A visitor to their workshops in 1898 reported that they had "a fine and complete library of the works of old designers" and that "old French styles of the periods of Louis XIV, XV, XVI and the Empire are much in request, especially of the period of Louis XV".[1] Plate 237.

This making of reproductions ±1900 was big business and highly respectable business. Gillows, as explained in Chapter 3, even opened a factory in Paris to ensure authenticity and claimed: "The old methods of weaving the Tapestries, of obtaining the marvellous colours and softness of the Marqueterie, the beautiful finish of the metal mounts (which are often cast from the original moulds) and the rich but subdued tone of the gilding, are followed in the most reverential spirit. Each piece is as perfect as the most expert craftsmanship can make it and equal to the original in everything save sentiment and historic interest. The work is often done by descendants of those who worked on the famous originals.

"We undertake commissions for the reproduction of any examples which our Clients may desire to possess and a practical test as to the faithfulness of these copies may be had by comparing pieces in our Galleries to the originals in the adjacent Wallace or Jones Collections."[2] It would be interesting to know if they were given the impressed 'Gillow' mark. It seems unlikely.

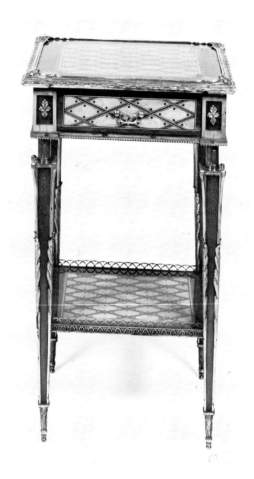

Plate 237. Ormolu mounted parquetry occasional table stamped Edwards and Roberts.

Hindley and Wilkinson of Welbeck Street and Old Bond Street argued persuasively in their preface that "There are many who appreciate the charm of old furniture but who are unwilling to expend the enormous sums of money asked for fine specimens. To such these reproductions are of great interest, for irrespective of the cost which is a tithe of that of the originals, the workmanship is in no way inferior and in appearance they possess just that old time-worn effect which gives such charm to the old work ... No pains are spared to collect the materials necessary for this in the nature of old wood for the frames, old velvets and embroideries, etc. for the covering, with a result which has frequently deceived the expert."[3] In other words: "Let us sell you repro but your guests will not be able to distinguish it from the genuine antique." Plates 238 and 239.

Firms at all levels were involved in the repro trade. J. Aldam Heaton, a top level designer and decorator supplied, c.1890-1900, 'Copies of Old Dressing Table Glasses much enlarged, the old ones being always far too small', 'the square back Adam and the Harp back Adam', both distinctly mean interpretations, a Queen Anne type jokily catalogued the 'Shaw' and handsome copies of black Venetian Mirrors with ripple wave mouldings and 'Old England Mirrors in vermilion and gilt'.[4] Plate 241 shows the middling firm of Trier & Co. advertising their reproductions. Gill and Reigate, dealers claiming "The largest stock of genuine antiques in London" announced, c.1910, "particular attention has been given to 'Reproductions'," that is "Modern Furniture exactly copied from the best designs of the sixteenth, seventeenth and eighteenth century makers."

High Wycombe manufacturers too were very involved. The *Cabinet Maker* in 1887 commended the manufacturer Edwin Skull for being "one of those who, happening to come across a nice old chair of attractive character and not unfitting for the present day has it carefully copied and thus, numerous old patterns are to be seen in his stock, mostly of solid and good Jacobean character and also pieces of furniture possessing an early genuine Queen Anne feeling". Similarly Frederick Parker was collecting desirable old specimens to inspire his firm (now the Parker Knoll Collection).

When the reformer C.R. Ashbee gave university extension lectures in High Wycombe in 1892 he chided the craftsmen for copying "old styles well enough — even to the worm holes". Certainly cabriole legged Windsors were being made at the beginning of the twentieth century.

Where now, most of a century of wear and distress later, are all these copies?

Advertisements in early issues of the *Connoisseur* from 1901 provide ample evidence of the mingling of genuine and reproduction pieces in the stock of reputable dealers.

Before considering intentional fakes there are two other categories worth mentioning:

1) Additional copies made to accompany genuine items

The spreading of a small set of chairs into six or eight or more by sharing out the legs is, of course, well known and there are the straightforward extras as in H.Golding's letter to the *Daily Mail* in December 1903: "A friend of mine had a genuine Chippendale chair and recently place it in a Bond Street firm's hand with instructions to make a dozen to match. This was done and a connoisseur found it difficult to say which was the original." At Carlton Towers, the Yorkshire home of the Duke of Norfolk, the dining room contains ten dining chairs made about 1740 and ten excellent copies made by Greenwoods of York late in the nineteenth century.

But single copies were sometimes made to create a pair of pier tables or commodes or, as here in 1912, when the wealthy collector H.C. Moffat bought a very elaborate late seventeenth century walnut, inlaid kneehole writing table ". . . for £336 12s from Messrs. Mallett at Bath" and "Mr. Mallett made a very excellent copy of it for himself and except for difference in the colour, the new was as good as the old. He told me it cost over £200 to make and I mention this to show that these specially fine pieces were as expensive to make then as they are now".[5]

2) Altered and/or 'improved' pieces

This is a large and complex category. Some items have been altered simply to meet changed needs as explained in this letter of 1891: "I send herewith a sketch of an old oak table which we have been restoring and cutting in two to make two side carving tables for the dining room of Scarisbrick Hall . . . Its size was 11ft. by 3ft."[6]

Other pieces have been improved or vandalised when their owners became hooked on carving, a specially prevalent addiction during this period, with many seat rails and table tops suffering.

But many pieces have been commercially 'improved' to render them more saleable as antiques. *The Pall Mall Gazette* reported in 1875 "These [eighteenth century] common chairs or tables or cabinets only need the addition of appropriate ornament and exhibition in a fashionable dealer's rooms to take rank and value as fine old Chippendale or marquetry furniture. There are many workmen in London who are mainly or wholly employed in 'enriching' goods from the old furniture market. The common oblong mahogany table that used to be found in every bedroom has an openwork 'gallery' added to its top and a veneering of fretwork glued round its edge. The useful mahogany sideboard which once existed in every 'parlour' had bands and medallions of satinwood judiciously inserted. The chairs or the cabinet which passes into the hands of the inlayer as a piece of unadorned mahogany or walnut comes out of them glowing in all the colours that nature or the dyer can give to woods. The vendor probably tells his customers but the truth. He says that the furniture is old and so it is. There is nothing new about it except the bits of decoration here and there, which do not make up a hundredth part of its bulk though they increase its price twenty fold."[7] Some very odd and improbable pieces must have resulted in this way and they are hardly likely to mislead informed purchasers.

Some 'improved' items can be found in historic houses. There is, for example, in Cumbria a famous set of chairs whose original back legs have been replaced below seat level by highly elaborate concoctions which echo the front legs and were probably made by the very skilful estate craftsman who is known to have worked in other rooms in the house early this century.

INTENTIONAL FAKING

The intentional faking of furniture has been a thriving business in England since at the latest the 1820s. It developed to feed appetites

Plate 238. Carved and gilt 'Louis XV' bergère armchairs made by Hindley and Wilkinson. Their catalogue states: "The chair [top] is covered with a genuine old brocade, forming a centre panel on the back and seat and margined with a rich old crimson silk velvet, embroidered with appliqué work. That [above] shows a similar arrangement with silk margins and corded embroidered work. As examples of Messrs. Hindley and Wilkinson's reproductions of old embroidery they cannot be surpassed." Early twentieth century.

147

Plate 239. Bureau du Roi, "an example par excellence of the important nature of Messrs. Hindley and Wilkinson's reproductions . . . It was recently executed by them to a special commission from the original . . . in the Louvre." That magnificent bureau was made by Riesener for Louis XV in 1769.

fostered by ideas and writers of the romantic movement and in particular by the works of Sir Walter Scott and his illustrators and by volumes such as Henry Shaw's *Ancient Furniture,* 1836, and Joseph Nash's *Mansions of England in the Olden Time*; 1839-49, all of which depicted mainly sixteenth and seventeenth century furnishings.

Loudon wrote in his great Encyclopaedia in 1833: ". . . we have now upholsterers in London who collect, both in foreign countries and in England whatever they can find of curious and ancient furniture, including fragments of fittings-up of rooms, altars and religious houses; and rearrange these curious specimens and adapt them to modern use", and "Wilkinson of Oxford Street and Hanson of John Street have extensive collections of Elizabethan and Dutch furniture and carvings, from which a judicious compiler of exteriors might clothe skeleton frames so as to produce objects of curiosity and interest at a very trifling expense. Kensett of Mortimer Street has also some curious specimens of both Elizabethan and more ancient furniture. Among these, we may mention a correct facsimile of a chair taken from Tintern Abbey, and now in Troy House, Monmouthshire; and two other chairs from Glastonbury; one of which, called the abbot's chair, is of very elaborate workmanship, and the other no less remarkable for the

Plate 240. Flamboyantly reproduced late seventeenth century type of lacquered cabinet on gilded stand, c.1900.

149

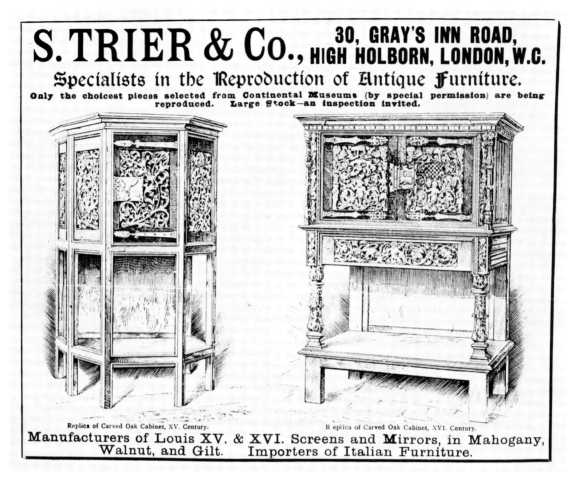

Plate 241. Advertisement of S. Trier & Co. who specialised in reproducing "the choicest pieces selected from Continental museums." Cabinet Maker, June 1892.

simplicity of its construction. Correct copies of these celebrated chairs are manufactured by Mr. Kensett for sale."[8] That was nearly a century and a half ago!

It was some of the early composite fake creations that were copied by ill-informed fakers at the end of the century.

H.B. Wheatley, the great recorder of the London scene, hinted in 1891: "Rumour says that the back premises of Wardour Street are largely devoted to the manufacture of antiques of all kinds."[9]

Arthur 'Chats on' Hayden revealed in 1905 ". . . it has been found that the foggy atmosphere in London is specially useful in producing the effect of age upon the finer [French made] work, consequently many forged pieces are shipped to London to be stored in order to ripen until considered fit for the American market where so many forgeries have been planted".[10]

Faking had continued to be profitable in France. André Mailfert claims in *Au Pays des Antiquaires* to have produced in Orleans between 1908 and 1930 seventy thousand 'rare old pieces' often from beams which he obtained when old houses were being demolished; but this implies the production of fifty items a week, so may be a tall story.

Plates 38 and 40 show examples of the work of the 'trade only' firm of Wainwright, probably of Hoxton, N.1., c.1880s onwards. Phrases like "convincingly antiqued very cleverly to represent old lacquer work" occur in their captions. But, of course, London did not have a monopoly of faking. There is the story of the lion-mask furniture faker of St. Albans and others had their own specialties.

150

Volume VII of *Modern Carpenter, Joiner and Cabinet Maker,* 1908, contained advice on the making of Japanese type cabinets on stands: "The cabinet itself is 3ft. square and is supported on a carved table 2½ft. high of Renaissance design. The cabinet is made of 1 inch material, with the exception of the back which is thinner. The interior which is closed by two doors, is fitted with a series of drawers of different sizes and separated from one another by ³⁄₈in. boards." The description ends: "Spanish and Queen Anne cabinets are frequently made to this pattern."

There is evidence of a much patronised early twentieth century London firm which gave good prices to impecunious historic country house owners for chairs from important documented sets and replaced them with good copies, so not all apparently documented items need be accepted without question.

Valuable insights into the kinds of pieces which have been faked can be gleaned from R.W. Symonds in *The Present State of old English Furniture* and his *English Furniture from Charles II to George II.*

Many fakers must have consulted the crop of detailed sketches and measured drawings published from c.1880 onwards. Of these, enquiring collectors might usefully consult:

L. André: Chests, Chairs, Cabinets and Old English Woodwork, 1879.

John W. Small: Ancient & Modern Furniture, 1883, limited to five hundred copies and much subscribed for by the trade.

W. Bliss Saunders: Examples of Carved Oak Woodwork in Houses & Furniture of 16th & 17th Centuries, 1883, has large diagrams of a much reproduced type of oak drawing table from Shibden Hall, Halifax.

Arthur Marshall: Specimens of Antique Carved Furniture and Woodwork, 1888.

Wm. Sharp Ogden: Examples of Antique Furniture, 1888; these had first appeared in twenty monthly parts, presumably for the trade.

Alfred E. Chancellor: Examples of Old Furniture, English & Foreign, 1898; these had been drawn for *The Building News.*

It is salutary and challenging to find the above architect Arthur Marshall warning in his preface, in 1888, that "As the difficulties of discriminating between the old work and the modern imitation become greater daily and the perfection which the imitators attain, render the difficulties still more marked; it is only by a careful study of drawings of old examples or the specimens themselves and by observing the harmony or embodiment of one idea which seems to pervade them, that we are enabled to form a correct judgment . . . we often see pieces of furniture — the framework of which may be genuine — but having carved panels introduced to replace plain ones, of a date and style quite out of keeping . . . I have known instances where the rusty heads of old nails have been forced into the holes made by new ones to conceal them . . . instances where the carving of 'made up' pieces of furniture has been covered with clay and brushed when dry, so that the sharp edge of the modern carving would be nicely softened off; the effect of the clay being also to produce somewhat similar appearance to an old barn door . . . Dates and names upon old furniture unless properly authenticated must be looked upon with the greatest suspicion. At a recent sale in the provinces a large number of examples were put up bearing the name and coat of arms of half the leading families in the county and most of them dated; however, the fact that so large a number of what purported to be valuable specimens should so suddenly become unearthed was sufficient evidence in itself against their being genuine. Spurious examples are often placed in the roadside cottages of Districts much frequented by tourists; and the deception is heightened by the story respecting their origin, that the tenant has off by heart."

For eighteenth century furniture, fakers had, of course, the inspiration of the great eighteenth century pattern books but how many copies were available at the craftsman's bench? Presumably most had to wait for magazine plates and nineteenth century reprints such as G.T. Thompson's *Designs of Chimney Glasses, Girandoles, Cabinets and Cornices after the style of Adam, Sheraton and Chippendale*, 1878, Batsford's edition of the *Architecture, Decoration and Furniture of R. & J. Adam*, 1881, a complete reprint of Sheraton's third edition in 1895 and the great two volumes in four of J. Aldam Heaton's *Furniture and Decoration of the 18th Century*, 1889.

Great skill certainly was expended by serious fakers. The writer and collector Constance Simon in 1907 passed on the story told by "a maker of reproductions on a somewhat large scale" that "when an exact copy had been made of an eighteenth century model the work was held over a fire of wood shavings until all the sharp edges and corners had been burned away. Lastly the piece was broken up into several parts and glued together again. Thus was the 'real antique' prepared for the market." [11] But the near impossibility of being able to suspend a piece of furniture over a fire at just the angle and for long enough to eliminate all the sharp edges, yet without damaging the piece enough to detract from its value, makes it seem likely that maybe that maker was deluding that writer.

Such care certainly cannot have been paid to individual items by a firm such as that of James C. Cawley of New Inn Yard, E.C., who along with seven others unselfconsciously appear under the heading 'Antique Furniture Manufacturers' in Kelly's Directory[12] in 1886: "Every description of English made, carved oak, walnut and mahogany furniture made to order . . . old work matched, etc., est. 1870" and "The only London maker [to the trade] of carved antique oak furniture, 2,000 chairs, easy chairs and settees in stock."

No, the really serious furniture faking must have been done by individuals or small workshops because of the need for secrecy. There are so many half told tales — of the East Anglian maker of champion Tompions, of the high quality Chippendale made in Lancashire at the turn of the century, of the pieces being given an impressed Gillow mark by a dealer in their own county NOW — and it is unlikely that there will be an end to the line of production.

To conclude: a warning against relying on written evidence. There was a story told in 1903 of a dealer who sold repro Chippendale to an earl who sent it to his country seat and had a connoisseur down to vet it. When the connoisseur scorned it the dealer agreed to take it back. The earl wrote on lordly crested paper: "I have this day sent you the furniture as arranged and shall thank you for the cheque forthwith." The dealer gleefully sent this apparent confirmation of authenticity to tempt an American collector adding, "You will see by the enclosed letter from Earl — that a very exceptional suite of fine Chippendale has come into my possession from — Castle, well worth £ — ."[13]

Caveat emptor

Footnotes

1. J.H. Bardwell and others, *Two Centuries of Soho, by the clergy of St Anne's,* 1898, p.185.
2. Gillow catalogue, *Examples of Furniture and Decoration,* c.1908, pub. Waring and Gillow, p.93.
3. Hindley and Wilkinson Ltd. catalogue, between 1900-12, probably later half of this period.
4. J. Aldam Heaton's catalogue, *Chimney Pieces, Glass, Decoration, Furniture,* 1890-1900.
5. H.C. Moffatt, *Illustrated description of some of the furniture at Goodrich Court, Herefordshire and Hampton Lodge, Wiltshire,* privately printed, OUP, 1928.
6. *Cabinet Maker,* Vol. 12, p.23, July 1891.
7. Quoted in R.W. Symonds and B.B. Whinneray, *Victorian Furniture,* 1962, p.54.
8. J.C. Loudon, *Encyclopaedia of Cottage, Farmhouse and Villa Architecture and Furniture,* 1833.
9. H.B. Wheatley, *London Past and Present,* 1891.
10. Arthur Hayden, *Chats on Old Furniture,* 1905, p.263.
11. Constance Simon, *English Furniture Designers of the 18th century,* 1907, p.199.
12. Kelly's Directory of Cabinet, Furniture and Upholstery Trades, 2nd edition, 1886.
13. *Building News,* Vol. 85, p.888, December 25, 1903.

CHAPTER 8

The Furniture Trade 1880~1915

ITS DISTRIBUTION, COMPOSITION, METHODS,
MECHANISATION AND PROFITABILITY

This is a vast topic needing detailed investigation; this chapter can only spotlight a few areas and aspects.

PREVIOUS DEVELOPMENTS

At the beginning of Victoria's reign small cabinet making businesses were well scattered throughout the kingdom. London's population of 1¾ million had one per 2,200 people, Bath and Colchester one per 1,000 and Norwich one per 1,650. The craftsmen in the cities and small towns supplied local needs and mainly made to order but London, Bath, Bristol, Leeds, Norwich and Edinburgh, at least, had some larger firms who, as in the eighteenth century, catered for distant country houses as well as city society and supplied some retailers in smaller towns with quality items and specialised goods.[1]

Between the Queen's accession in 1837 and 1880 the population of England and Wales increased by two thirds and that of Scotland by half to a total of nearly 30 million. The industrial cities were expanding rapidly but even so, in 1881 Lancashire, the county with by far the largest cities and population, numbered less than 3½ million, so London with nearly 4 million vastly outdistanced all the other cities.

Cabinet making had been a craft industry relying on handwork except for such components as could be shaped by the mechanical saws and lathes of the steam powered saw mills. But as firms and numbers grew with the population explosion, and certainly from the middle of the century, there was more mechanisation of more than preliminary processes. Holland & Sons spent £1,250 in 1857 on machinery for vertical and circular sawing, fret cutting and mortising at their Ranelagh Works, Pimlico.[2] Another prestige firm, Jackson & Graham, advertised in 1862 that in their "extensive Manufactory adjoining, the Machinery, worked by Steam Power, is fitted with all means and appliances to insure superiority and economize cost," [3] and in the 1870s they were actually designing with a view to machine production. Some idea of the size to which a few firms had grown can be gauged from the fact that Jacksons employed between 600 and 1,000 men, including decorators, at peak times in the 70s.[4]

Inside a Wycombe chair factory, 1902.
Courtesy E. Sweetland.

First steam lorry used to transport chairs from Wycombe to London. On its maiden trip it carried 700 chairs at a speed of 6 m.p.h., March 1903. Courtesy E. Sweetland.

Loading chairs on the horse-drawn wagons at Gibbons Factory, High Wycombe, c.1895. These wagons usually carried 200-300 chairs per trip. Courtesy Ronald Goodearl.

But most cabinet makers still worked in very small businesses and the majority had come to be concentrated in London by 1880 and mainly in the East End.

The trade's rapid development there must have been due not only to the favourable rail, canal and port facilities and convenient timber yards and lower rents but also, especially, to the very active and forceful East End wholesalers who bought and were able to sell the products of these thousands of small makers to many regions at home and overseas. This wholesale trade must have been greatly helped by being so very close to the Shoreditch original 1839 terminus of the EC Railway; and when the line was extended to Liverpool Street in 1875 the old terminus became, most conveniently, Bishopsgate Goods Station.

More than forty specialised trades had come to be involved in furniture production from spring makers, medieval ironmongers and veneer cutters to upholsterers and twine manufacturers.

DISTRIBUTION AND COMPOSITION OF THE TRADE 1880-1915

OUTLINE OF DISTRUBUTION IN 1880s

Census returns provide the astonishing information that in 1881 more than two thirds of the cabinet makers of England and Wales were working in London and mainly in the north east of it. The rest were distributed throughout the country and only a few places were specially noted for furniture making. Some cities and certainly Bath, Bristol, Edinburgh, Glasgow, Leeds, Liverpool, Manchester, Newcastle-on-Tyne, Norwich, Salisbury and Warwick each had makers of international exhibition standard and Lancaster had long had the fine Gillow factory. High Wycombe was by far the largest centre of chair making with Addingham in Yorkshire, Chipping and some towns in Lancashire, Macclesfield in Cheshire and Worksop in Nottinghamshire among other places specialising in chairs but on a lesser scale. Some bamboo, cane and wicker furniture was made in London and Manchester but the specialised centres of production were Birmingham for bamboo, Leicester and Nottingham for wicker. Metal furniture was produced in Birmingham, which specialised in beds, and in Manchester, London and Glasgow.

But less known facts are revealed in a London made survey of 1888: "Beith near Glasgow is said to be a rival of London in high class furniture, leaving inferior goods to London. A few years ago there were only fifty who made furniture there, now there are five hundred; and I am further told that Alnwick supplies the largest London houses with best goods and that 50% of our high class furniture comes from Scotland and the West of England and that Barnstaple pays the best prices for designs." [5]

Thus although London's production was great enough to supply many in the provinces and was exported "to all climes," it was supplemented by advantageous purchases from specialised centres in Scotland and the provinces.

London and the rest of the country will now be considered separately. For easier reference and so as not to delay the story of the trade, the names of firms in each category are printed at the end of the chapter.

LONDON 1880-1915

WEST END: RETAILERS AND MAKERS

All districts had some small makers and retailers but the top quality furniture firms were still mainly in W.1, particularly in Bond Street, Mount Street, Regent Street, Berners Street, Oxford Street and around Baker Street. These firms made a good deal of their stock in their own workshops. Perhaps because Victoria's reign had not produced any great pattern books, it became customary from the 1860s for big firms to employ designers[6] and at first these were mainly French.

The Booth Survey[7] in 1889 reported "The importance of West End shops in the trade has declined for some years and there are few, if any, employing more than fifty men when busy" but "the men working in these shops are the pick of the trade. The trade is so varied that two articles are seldom made alike and each workman must be able to carry a job right through, working to a pattern or drawing and, it may be at the same time, introducing some modification that is required. The work is always supposed to be done entirely by hand but the influence of the more rapid methods of machinery begins to make itself felt." A worker's guide in the 80s pointed out that "the chief upholsterers and furniture makers are particular about their workmen and it is not easy to procure work at Gillows, Jackson & Graham and houses of their standing."[8] Jacksons employed a good many foreign craftsmen for marquetry and inlay.

Some goods were made for these firms by the 'piece-masters' in the Tottenham Court Road area. These piece-masters did not usually employ more than twenty workers. Learners and improvers did a lot of the work but there were also specialist polishers, carvers and fret cutters equipped with mechanical circular, band and felt saws. Many craftsmen from Scotland and the provinces came to work there to gain experience of London ways.

MECHANISATION

Exactly when part mechanisation became a significant factor in furniture making in the West End is not clear, but certainly by the 1860s Jackson & Graham and Holland & Sons were making considerable use of machinery and it seems unlikely that Gillows and other major firms would have been slow to follow. One of the machines was probably 'Sketchley's Universal Joiner' whose maker in Weymouth advertised in 1867: "This machine has been awarded Two Medals. It is acknowledged to be the first before the Trade by Builders and others who have them at work. It will saw 20″ deep, plane 11″, mould 5″ wide, tenon, rebate, groove, bore and converts timber and deals into any shape."[9] In 1867 too, there was news of a new machine invented by "Mr. Robert Thompson, late engineer in charge of the wood-working machinery at HM Dockyard, Woolwich." His machinery was "readily adapted for cutting curvilinear and other shaped mouldings in wood and also finishing and polishing the same ... and will accomplish as much work as 25 skilled workmen in the same period of time."[10]

Four hole borer for Windsor seats, c.1890. A good hand craftsman could probably bore the seats as quickly as this machine, but the machine reduced physical effort and also brought a type of work, previously the prerogative of the craftsman, into the scope of the semi-skilled machine-hand.
Courtesy Wycombe Chair Museum.

A twisting lathe, c.1886. The twists produced still needed finishing by hand, and 'cleaning twists' was a regular occupation.
Courtesy Wycombe Chair Museum.

Drawing of the premises of the Midland Furnishing Co. Ltd., Southampton Row, Holborn, W.C.

SALES PUBLICITY

The West End firms were patronised because of their well earned reputations, but trade was not too brisk and they found it necessary to woo old customers and a wider clientele with lavish literature and exhibitions. Increasingly large and elaborate catalogues became a feature of late nineteenth century marketing. Oetzmanns catalogue of c.1897 included reprints of magazine articles by M.F. Frith on *How to Furnish a House for £250 and £120.* Gillows early twentieth century catalogues were bound coffee table tomes, and Hindley & Wilkinson's a hard backed large quarto volume with excellent mounted photographs. Plates 24-26.

As early as 1862 Jackson & Graham had advertised their 27,000 square feet of "spacious showrooms and galleries" [11] and Gillows had "very spacious and handsomely fitted up showrooms" in 1881 and probably much earlier. The *Ladies Field,* presumably copying a press hand-out, reported on their large permanent Exhibition Galleries of reproductions in March 1903: "It may at first be thought rather curious to say that Gillows showrooms are more instructive to those interested in the decorative arts than the great Museums ... but it must be remembered that while the Museums almost entirely satisfy themselves with collecting authentic pieces, Gillows collection has been brought together with the view of representing a complete and comprehensive stock. Although the Museums, therefore, have specimens of great individual beauty their collections are more or less disjointed whilst the Gillow rooms contain a range of subjects literally illustrating the history of decoration through every period worthy of notice." [12] Judging from the range of contracts Gillows obtained, this lavish display did stimulate 'can't-wait-to-get-it-home' feelings and pay dividends.

SUPPLIES

What the West End shops did not make for themselves they bought from:
1) the increasing number of small specialised makers or piece-masters around Tottenham Court Road and Euston.
2) the quality factories like Smees in Finsbury and Dyer & Watts in Islington.
3) some of the reputable makers like G.S. Lucraft and J.S. Henry in the East End.
4) quality producers in Scotland and the provinces.

But by the end of this period many of these fine firms had vanished or merged or been absorbed by the new department stores. This was due, perhaps, to a falling off in demand for top quality work and partly to the more pushing, active selling of the big stores and house furnishers like Whiteley 'the Universal Provider' and Harrods which offered everything from "ebonised cabinets, lead lined coffins and coal @ 2/- a ton to stable requisites for horses with long feet."

HOUSE FURNISHERS AND DEPARTMENT STORES

In addition to the temptations of their vastly detailed catalogues these big stores provided imaginative and helpful displays. A visitor to Whiteleys in 1880 reported it was "crammed with stock but no confusion ... " The floor devoted to bedroom furniture was arranged according to quality starting with ten piece bedroom suites at

£5.7s.6d., "they range consecutively round the walls up to 150 guineas ... customers can be their own salesmen; they can compare qualities side by side ... without being worried into buying things more costly than they desire."[13] Whiteleys seem to have been the first to show completely fitted up 'rooms' in their windows in 1882. When in 1887 the custom developed of showing prices in the windows conservative members of the trade feared this would lead to unhealthy competition.

Whiteleys and some furnishing stores had workshops where some furniture was made but they were mainly 'finishing' shops for the upholstering, polishing and glass fitting of articles bought cheaply 'in the white'. They no doubt, at first bought much from the big wholesalers in and around Curtain Road and Great Eastern Street but gradually many of the East End garret-masters (who supplied those wholesalers) and the piece-masters around Tottenham Court Road became better organised and sold direct to the big stores. Unfortunately, the many opportunities for 'contracting out' or 'sweating' enabled the big stores to set one small maker against another and even against their own workmen. Maples, in the late 80s, said they bought from a thousand different suppliers and it was generally thought that they made less than ten per cent of what they sold. They ordered and paid weekly so most of their suppliers worked locally. Plate 242 provides evidence of Jas. Shoolbred, also of Tottenham Court Road, buying sideboards made by the Alnwick firm of T. Robertson & Sons in 1882.

At the beginning of this period there were a few quality shops like these and Heals in Tottenham Court Road, but in general the street had a poorish reputation until by the late 80s its standards had risen and trade there was then at its zenith for nearly a couple of decades. How fine and extensive some of this was can be gauged from the resulting furore when in 1903 the Viceroy of India, Lord Curzon, opening an Exhibition of Indian Art in Delhi, warned Indian princes to abjure the productions of Tottenham Court Road. Sir John Blundell Maple thundered telegraphically that he had furnished palaces for the Kings of Siam and Portugal, the Durbar Room of the Maharajah of Mysore and supplied carpets and chairs to the Viceroy's own lodge in Calcutta; [14] whilst *The Telegraph* vouched "...Tottenham Court Road is now the great furniture market of the country ... everything is supplied to meet the wants and tastes of the crowned heads and the suburban householder."

EAST END: WHOLESALERS AND MAKERS

COMPOSITION OF THE TRADE

It was during this period that the East End came to supersede the West End as the main centre of production in the metropolis. The 1881 census shows c.12,000 men and 3,000 women and boys were engaged in cabinet making in Shoreditch, Bethnal Green, Hackney and Tower Hamlets. The trade there in the last decades of the century consisted of:
— very many small makers or garret-masters employing perhaps three to six workers.
— a score or so of workshops employing a score or so of men and producing best furniture. Plate 243.

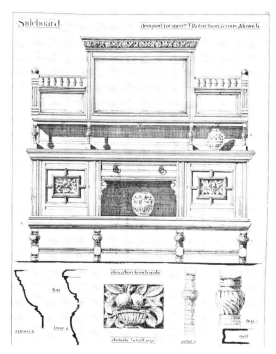

Plate 242. John Small's Plate 33, a sideboard designed for Robertson and Son of Alnwick, "had a great success in the market". It appeared in the Shoolbred catalogue in 1882.

Plate 243. Advertisement by J.S. Henry showing a cosy corner fitment. Henry prided himself on being way ahead with his 'novelties' and on supplying only to the trade. It is interesting that he here refers to himself as 'designer'. Cabinet Maker, June 1892.

- thirty five to forty workshops, also with about twenty men making rather poorer goods and probably specialising in bedroom and/or dining room furniture.
- three or four factories employing 50-190 or so workers and producing cheapest to good work, e.g. H. Herrmann Ltd. of City Road — "the largest manufacturers of bedroom suites in Europe". Plate 244 shows their Limehouse factory in 1891. The Dyer's factory was in Islington.
- lastly a dozen or so large wholesalers who, like W. Bailey (Plate 246), were themselves manufacturers but also bought a great deal from the garret-masters. Most of the wholesalers were in Curtain Road, Great Eastern Street and City Road.[15]

There was a certain amount of immigrant labour, especially Russians and Germans and some Poles and Jews. Although in 1888 there were only two hundred members of the Hebrew Cabinet Makers' Association, their number increased and for some reason many of them specialised in bedroom furniture.

It was said at the time that the trade was made up of "wage earning slaves, driven and driving garret-masters and powerful, wealthy wholesalers". This was largely true because most workmen and small garret-masters were at the mercy of the wholesalers since they led a hand to mouth existence often needing to sell their products before they could afford to buy wood to make more; and whilst not all wholesalers were always greedy, grasping characters wanting to buy at unfair prices, the trade depressions of 1873-86 had created "a universally increased keenness and prevailing demand for cheapness". Some garret-masters, no doubt, had reasonably satisfactory arrangements and some of the better organised began to supply West End and

Plate 244. The new H. Herrmann Steam Factory in Dod Street, Limehouse, London, E. Timber was delivered by boat. They specialised in hard wood bedroom suites including "the handsome ash-burr suites brought out last spring." Cabinet Maker, *October 1891.*

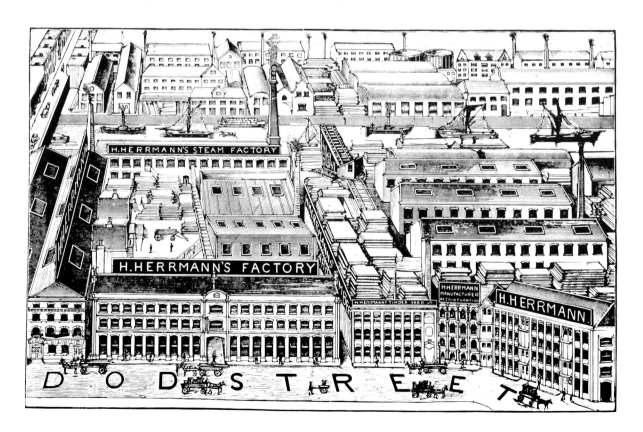

Plate 245. *Bird's eye view of the layout of the warehouse and factories of "T. Lawes and Co. cabinet makers, upholsterers, timber and feather merchants, bedding, looking glass and pianoforte manufacturers."* Cabinet Maker, *November 1882.*

Wholesale Cabinet and Looking Glass Manufacturers.
102, and in rear of 104, 106, 108 & 110, CURTAIN ROAD, LONDON, E.C.
VISIT, OR SAMPLE ORDERS EARNESTLY SOLICITED.

ESTABLISHED 1825.   TELEPHONE No. 131.

Substantial Artistic Furniture at most moderate prices for the Drawing Room, Dining Room, Bed Room, Boudoir, Library, and Office.

Drawing Room Suites in Tapestry and Plush, from £5 5s. 0d. to £100.

Dining Room Suites in Leather or Utrecht Velvet, from £9 10s. 0d. to £50.

Walnut Pianofortes, fullCompass from £11 10s 0d. to £60, extraordinary value at £23 10s 0d. & £35.

Bed Room Suites, complete in serviceable decorated Deal, from £3 15s. 0d. In American Walnut, from £10 15s 0d to £90. In Ash, from £9 15s. 0d

Office Pedestal Tables, 4ft. with 9 Drawers and LeatherTop in Oak, Walnut, or Mahogany, from 56s. to

Dining Tables, with Patent Screw, complete from 25s.

Sideboards, bevelled plate, 6ft., from £6 15s. 0d. to £50.

W. B. & S., 6449.

No. 6448.—OVERMANTEL, 4 ft. 9 in. high by 5 ft. 3 in. wide, projecting centre plate, 20 plates - - - £10 5 0
No. 6449.—MANTELPIECE - - - - - - - - - - - £8 10 0 -£18 15 0

Plate 246. Advertisement by the old established Curtain Road wholesalers William Bailey & Son in Kelly's *Directory of Cabinet Furniture and Upholstery Trades, 1886.*

other retailers direct; but there was great economic insecurity and much heart-rending distress. There are many accounts of "chamber (garret) masters and workmen who make on spec, have to hawk their goods in Curtain Road on Saturdays and are miserably taken advantage of". Makers who did not have facilities to polish, upholster or fit their products with glass or mirrors were the most vulnerable as there was little bargaining power in unfinished goods like chair frames or chests of drawers 'in the white'.

The survey by J.B. Lakeman in 1888 reported that "wages in London for skilled makers have fallen 33% in sixteen years. . . . . For many years past no apprentices have been taken on in the low class of goods; boys will not learn the trade nor will such masters employ their sons because the work is now so poorly paid . . ."[16]

Perhaps though, there was an element of independence and erratic gaiety as the report continues "Mondays and Tuesdays are saint days and during the other four days work continues till late at night". Obviously there was much irregularity but the average working week was 52-56 hours.

Although close to Curtain Road, the established Finsbury factories like Smees "where men are as highly skilled and as well paid as any in West End houses" seem to have been mainly apart from its wholesaling.[17] Plate 247.

Thus all grades of furniture were produced in the East End from "the richly inlaid cabinet" that may be sold for £100 or the carved chair that can be made to pass as rare 'antique' workmanship to gipsy tables at 9s. a dozen.

The survey by J.B. Lakeman in 1888 reported that "wages in

HAND PRODUCTION AND MECHANISATION IN THE EAST END

Although mechanisation was introduced into the few East End factories and some of the larger workshops, most of the cheapest furniture continued to be made mainly by hand because labour was cheap and the small garret-masters did not have the capital to install machinery. These small makers were able to manage with only hand

MOORE AND HUNTON,
WHOLESALE AND EXPORT
CABINET MAKERS AND UPHOLSTERERS,
59 to 64, Worship Street & 107 to 112, Paul Street,
FINSBURY SQUARE, LONDON, E.C.
DINING, DRAWING AND BEDROOM SUITES.
Chippendale, Queen Anne, Early English, and Renaissance Styles.
The Warehouses are close to Moorgate Street, Broad Street and Liverpool Street Termini.
NEW ILLUSTRATED CATALOGUE SENT POST FREE. [22]

Plate 247. Advertisement showing premises of the Finsbury Square wholesalers Moore and Hunton. With buildings of this size they presumably made most of their own stock. Kelly's *Directory of Cabinet Furniture and Upholstery Trades, 1886.*

160

tools in their workshops because the East End had three or four steam powered saw mills where the sections and shapes they required could be cut for them. The owners of these saw mills were timber merchants who used the steam power to cut logs into planks but they leased steam power and bench room to sawyers who, with band and circular saws and fret cutters, cut the shapes required by the furniture makers. In one large mill thirty sawyers worked for the owners and a hundred and fifty others worked in rented spaces. Turners too rented powered bench rooms and thus were able to supply vast quantities of spindles very cheaply, a factor which helps to explain the spread of 'spindle mania' in the 1880s.

There are not as yet many clues as to when East End factories became mechanised. It has been assumed that because of the availability of cheap labour they were slow to install expensive machinery, but as snippets of evidence come to light it begins to seem unlikely that they lagged behind those in the West End. It was reported in 1869, for example, of W. Walker & Sons of Bunhill Row, E.C.2, who specialised in the production of good quality gothic furniture, that "the establishment is large and complete. Appliances of all kinds exist for saving labour and advantages are to be found which can only be offered by the combination of skill, capital and organization."[18]

SALES PUBLICITY

To attract retailers, the wholesalers had to send out very comprehensive catalogues. Perhaps the first of these had been the sturdy great volume issued by W. & A. Smee in the middle of the century. It was customary before 1880 to show items only in elevation but after W. Walker & Sons then issued their *New Design Books* in perspective, explaining "It is so very difficult to get the uninitiated to understand at a glance the drawings made after furniture trade fashion", perspective came to be the accepted form.

In 1886 J.T. Norman, the wholesaler of Great Eastern Street, offered a handsome two hundred page illustrated catalogue complete with retail prices and the retailer's name printed on the cover so that a shop could pretend to be offering its own make when actually being supplied by Norman. Whilst William Bailey, Sloper & Co., old established Curtain Road-ers, went one step further in 1899 offering, in return for guaranteed orders, five hundred or a thousand free copies, printed with the retailer's name and address, of *Up-to-Date Design Book T* which retailers could then distribute as their own catalogue.[19]

One of the very largest must surely have been the 1,080 page catalogue about 1900 by S. and S. (Sewell & Sewell) of London Wall. A surviving copy has the name of the retailer 'J. Leng & Son, Eastgate, Chichester' printed in gilt on the binding.[20]

But many retailers must have relied on the series of Furniture Trade Catalogues published by the *Furniture Gazette* in the 80s. . . . "in the hope that it may become the Standard work of Reference for the trade throughout the country supplying as it does the acknowledged want of an Illustrated Price List of modern Furniture of the style in general demand and such as can be purchased at any large Wholesale house". Armed with this book of designs and its price list, a retailer, knowing the illustrated items were available from wholesalers, could offer a

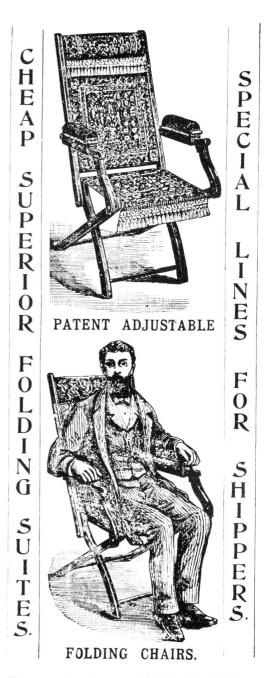

CHEAP SUPERIOR FOLDING SUITES.

SPECIAL LINES FOR SHIPPERS.

PATENT ADJUSTABLE

FOLDING CHAIRS.

From an advertisement of 1898 of the Hackney manufacturing firm of H. Baverstock.

customer a wide choice even though his own stock might be small. Plates 8 to 10 are from Furniture Trade Catalogues.

But by 1904 wholesalers were finding buyers increasingly reluctant to select from catalogues and so their salesmen had to carry more and more samples.

SCOTLAND AND THE PROVINCES

MAKERS

The London oriented *Cabinet Maker* admitted, December 1, 1880: "It is difficult to convince those who have only moved in the London furniture market that the provinces can successfully compete with the Metropolis in the design and production of art furniture. . . . but. . . . the productions of good provincial cabinet makers often evince more originality of design than their London rivals."[21] There were in the provinces firms like James Lamb of Manchester and Marsh, Jones & Cribb of Leeds capable of producing very high quality furniture for exhibitions and local prestige contracts. Robsons of Newcastle-on-Tyne, "the largest and most complete house furnishing establishment in the North of England", had the contract to furnish Benwell Towers, the new palace of the Bishop of Newcastle and Caleb Trapnell of Bristol furnished the Assize Courts and Mansion House there, whilst the locally respected firm of Arthur Foley of Salisbury had "a somewhat more extended reputation as a wholesale manufacturer principally of bedroom suites".[22]

But it was Beith, Bath and Barnstaple which were cited in the Lakeman survey as specially notable provincial centres of cabinet making in the 80s.

SCOTLAND

Beith's growth was remarkable but perhaps not all that surprising as it is close to Glasgow which had long been well supplied with cabinet makers.[23]

There were nearly 170 businesses in Glasgow in 1886. Then Beith, with a population of only 4,000, had one cabinet maker and two wholesale firms: M. & J. Pollock and Robert Balfour (founded 1860), 'Art Furniture Manufacturer & West of Scotland Chair Factory'. By 1894 the town's population had grown to 7,000 and it had seven wholesalers including Balfours, who in 1893 had advertised themselves as "the largest and best equipped cabinet factory in Scotland" with a branch in Glasgow and a London office off Cheapside.

It was reported of Wylie & Lochhead, one of the foremost Glasgow firms in 1882, that they had recently erected as cabinet works . . . "one of the most complete buildings of its kind in Europe . . . A capital marine engine of one hundred horse power keeps the machinery of the establishment in motion . . . a multitude of wood-working machines . . . and all the recent appliances for planing, ploughing, tonguing, mortising, tenoning, etc., were to be seen in action.

"The fitting and furnishing of some of the finest Clyde built steamers comes into the hands of this firm and they specially cultivate such a class of trade. The carving on some of the saloon easy chairs and settees was boldly executed and indeed the carving shop contains not a few men who can wield the chisel with rare skill. In passing through the cabinet making department one feature naturally strikes any observer

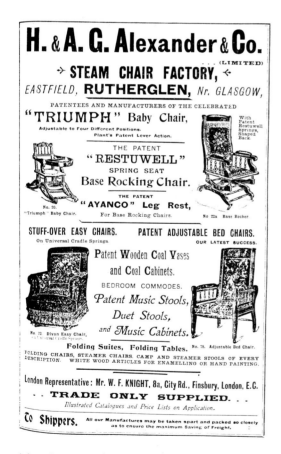

Advertisement for a steam chair factory in Scotland from Kelly's Directory, 1903.

accustomed to southern work, i.e. the substance of the material employed and the thoroughness of the work. . . . some of the wardrobes we saw in process of making would weigh down many a complete bedroom suite of London make.

". . . . everything is undertaken on the premises from the caning of a five shilling chair to the silvering of plate glass and including the gilding of the looking glass frames."[24]

They catered also for death with "rows of costly and magnificent hearses, exquisite carriages and hundreds of horses". They employed about 1,700 workers.

Edinburgh had a long tradition of cabinet making and trade had probably been stimulated by Queen Victoria ordering furniture for Balmoral from several makers there. Twenty four Edinburgh firms subscribed to John Small's *Ancient and Modern Furniture* in 1883 but there is little evidence to suggest that production there was on a large scale. Kirkcaldy had the growing firm of A.H. Mackintosh & Co. established in 1860.

BARNSTAPLE

Barnstaple had the notable firm Shapland & Petter, 'Art and Bedroom, Moulding and Wainscot Manufacturing Cabinet-Makers, wholesale cabinet turners and Hardwood, Mahogany and veneer merchants,' and five other makers and one 'antique furniture manufacturer' in 1894.

BATH

In 1886 Bath had three wholesale manufacturers, forty three other cabinet makers plus, after 1894, Bath Cabinet Makers who made good quality progressive furniture. Plate 108.

Other noted makers in the West Country were Wake & Dean at Yatton in Somerset and Smith & Co. in Bristol.

LANCASTER

Lancaster with its Gillow factory had been an important centre of quality furniture making since the later part of the eighteenth century. By the end of the nineteenth it was highly mechanised, as described on p.168, and very, very productive in many styles.

ALNWICK

The Alnwick firm already mentioned as supplying high class work to London was Thomas Robertson & Sons, 'Cabinet Maker, Wholesale Chair & Dining Table Manufacturers, House Furnishers and Timber Merchants'. Like Balfours they bought designs from the Edinburgh architect John Small. Plate 242.

HIGH WYCOMBE: chair making and cabinet making

High Wycombe was the largest furniture making centre in the provinces, specialising in chairs but also producing cabinet work. Chairmaking had been an important trade there since the eighteenth century. By 1875 there were fifty chair manufacturers and five of them: Birch, Cartwright, Cox, Glenister & Gibbons, and Edwin Skull employed more than fifty workers. By the 80s they and others had

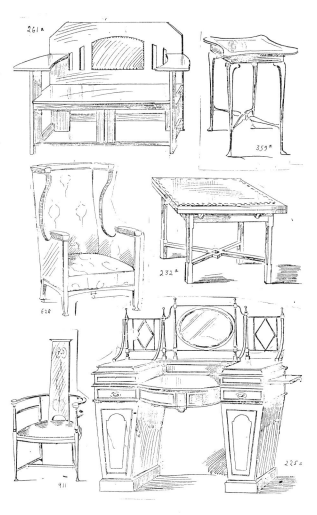

Plate 248. These items from a cost and design book of the High Wycombe firm of William Birch show the diversity of its products. They seem to have been one of the largest provincial makers of progressive furniture.

163

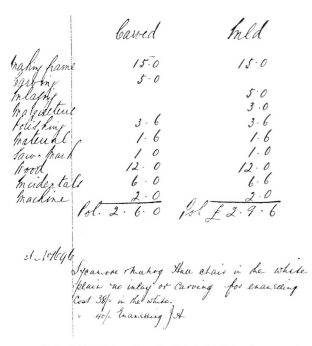

	Carved	Inld
making frame	15.0	15.0
carving	5.0	
Inlaying		5.0
marqueterie		3.0
polishing	3.6	3.6
material	1.6	1.6
saw mark	1.0	1.0
wood	12.0	12.0
incidentals	6.0	6.6
machine	2.0	2.0
	Tot. 2.6.0	Tot £2.9.6

1/10/96

Sycamore mahog Hall chair in the white plain no inlay or carving for enamelling Cost 38/= in the white.
" 40/= Enamelling JH.

Plate 249. This estimate dated 21.2.1., for an oak hall chair, carved or inlaid, from a William Birch cost and design book shows how carefully each material and process was costed.

Plate 249. This estimate dated 21.2.1 for an oak hall chair, carved or inlaid, from a William Birch cost and design book shows how carefully each material and process was costed.

expanded. Some mechanisation and much specialisation by bodgers or turners, chair bottomers, assemblers, caners and rushers ensured a vast output. In the mid 70s, 19,200 chairs were rapidly supplied to the Sankey & Moody evangelical campaigns and a factory inspector in 1888 estimated the town's production at 1,800 dozen, that is, over 21,000 chairs a week. They varied from simple mission chairs at 1s. each via ordinary lath backs and Roman spindles and rocking and folding steamer chairs to high quality cabriole leggled, pierced splat Windsors and rosewood framed fancy and gossip chairs, Plate 22. The *Cabinet Maker* reported in June 1886 that Glenister & Son concentrated on high quality goods, that Benjamin North was the largest maker in all grades of chair making, that William Birch had one of the smartest, largest and best managed factories in the town and produced work of the highest class and with inlay. Charles Skull, having succeeded his father, was complimented on "having successfully departed from the stereotyped class of Wycombe chair"[25] with his new lines in 'gossip' and fancy chairs. Wycombe certainly prospered from the 80s by responding to fashion's challenge for a great variety of fancy chairs for the drawing room instead of the old 'matching set of nine'.

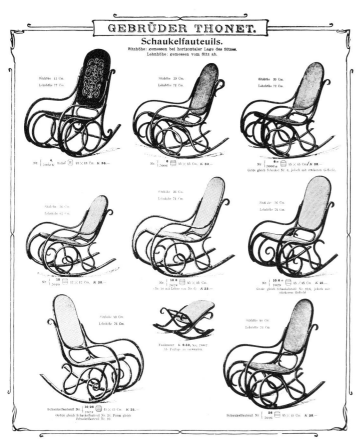

Plate 250. Page from Gebrüder Thonet catalogue, 1904.

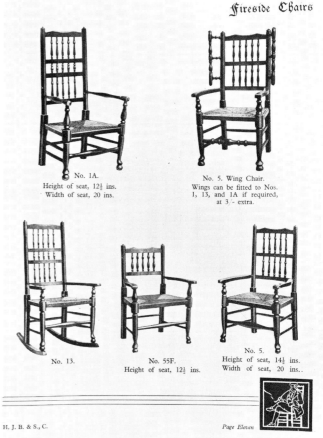

Plate 251. This page from a 1930s catalogue of the firm of H.J. Berry of Chipping, Lancashire, shows traditional examples which had been in production since the nineteenth century.

An interesting High Wycombe contract was that from the Office of Works, in 1902, for 2,000 cane seated stools and 600 mahogany, rush seated chairs for peers and peeresses at the Coronation of Edward VII. The majority of these chairs were supplied by Glenisters at 24s. each.[26]

But several firms including Nicholls and Janes Ltd. and Birch began to make a wide range of cabinet goods in addition to chairs. There is a report of 1887[27] that inlaid suites in mahogany and rosewood produced 'in the white' at Birch's Wycombe factory were brought to London to receive the finishing touches in the way of stuffing, covering and polishing at the firm's new premises in Euston Road. Their sketch books show a wide range of items and types, represented here by Plates 161-164 and Plate 249 from an estimates book, shows how carefully each material and process was costed.

Benjamin North also had premises in London in the 90s. The very important firm of Nicholls and Janes Ltd. had a high reputation for largely handmade quality reproductions of 'Elizabethan, Jacobean, Stuart, Queen Anne, Georgian, Regency, Victorian ....' They also specialised in smaller items like globes, stools, stands and carvings and made the furniture designed by Sir Edwin Lutyens.

High Wycombe certainly suffered competition from Austrian bentwood furniture makers, especially Thonets, whose splendid multilingual catalogue of 1904 offered many challenges (Plate 250), but it continued to be the main provincial centre of furniture making.

LESSER CENTRES OF CHAIRMAKING

CHIPPING, Lancashire

Chairs have been crafted in Chipping since, certainly, the 1840s, but around 1900 production was greatly expanded by the Berry family who

Plate 252. A Worksop made 'Roman spindle' chair, heavier than its Wycombe namesake and with its distinctive turning and button polish finish. The notched curved ends of the top rail are a Worksop characteristic c.1900.

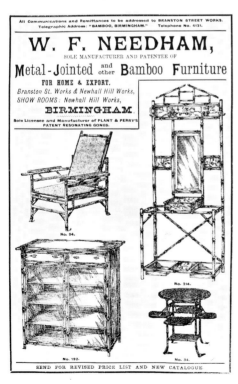

Plate 253, left. Advertisement of W.F. Needham, Birmingham, bamboo furniture manufacturer, in Kelly's Directory of Cabinet Furniture and Upholstery Trades, 1886.

Plate 254, right. Advertisement of W.T. Ellmore & Son, Leicester, willow furniture manufacturer in Kelly's Directory of Cabinet Furniture and Upholstery Trades, 1889.

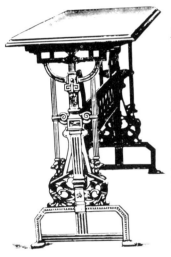

Plate 255. Top and centre, cast iron 'Pastimes' table and bottom the 'W.G. Grace' made by Bennett's Ironfoundry Co., Ardwick, Manchester, "suppliers of round and square tables for restaurants, hotels, coffee taverns, tea gardens, parlours and occasional tables and flower stands for drawing rooms etc." Cabinet Maker, *Vol. 12, p.248, 1892.*

ever since have specialised in varieties of spindle back and other rush seated chairs. Plate 251.

WORKSOP, Nottinghamshire

Worksop had had chairmakers since at least the 1830s but by the 80s there were largish firms, notably Isaac Allsop & Sons until c.1890 and W. Gilling & Sons until c.1914. Worksop chairs were Windsors but of rather more generous proportions and more highly finished than many Wycombe chairs. They had more robust spindles and these and legs were elaborately and distinctively turned as in Plate 252. Many were in cherry wood with elm seats. The notched curved ends of the top rail are a Worksop characteristic.

ADDINGHAM, Yorkshire

Addingham had the woodworking firm of W. Brears & Son who among many other domestic and agricultural items produced Windsor chairs from c.1860 until the 1930s. Christopher Gilbert explains: "They were inexpensive smokers bows, spindle and lath back chairs, base rockers, simple children's chairs, kitchen and hotel stools, towel rails and walking stools or go-carts. All were very cheap (high back Windsors @ 8/-, spindle back kitchen chairs at 42/- per dozen, small round stools 6/- per dozen, c.1900) made of native timber although available in walnut or mahogany to order and extremely conservative in design. The catalogues record that large consignments were supplied for workhouses, schools, refreshment rooms, hospitals, concert halls, clubs and public houses. . . . many turned chairs were sent to Manchester".[28]

WICKER, CANE AND BAMBOO FURNITURE

Bamboo furniture was made by Eli Frampton in Manchester and many firms in London but the Midlands attracted the largest makers of bamboo, wicker and cane items. Birmingham was the centre for bamboo with the Mikado Bamboo Co. and Wm. Frederick Needham, offering the widest selection. Plate 253. Leicester had W.T. Ellmore and Son (Plate 254) claiming in 1899 to be "the largest manufacturers in willow and cane in Europe"; whilst Morris & Wilkinson & Co. of Nottingham countered with the claim of being "the largest wicker manufacturer in the Kingdom."

METAL FURNITURE

Birmingham was the old established centre of the metal bedstead making industry but the enterprising Horatio Myer set up in Vauxhall, S.E., in 1876 and was soon a major supplier in London and the south. Plate 198. Bennett's Ironfoundry, Manchester were large suppliers of metal tables such as 'The Pastimes' pattern and the 'W.G. Grace' with heads of W.G. on each leg. Plate 255.

EXTENT OF DELIVERIES

Neither the London and provincial wholesalers nor their retailer customers appear to have been deterred by the complications and cost of long distance delivery. The extent of exports from Scotland to London has been stressed but there was a reverse trend with, for example, Wylie & Lochhead of Glasgow buying the 'Saxon'[29] as well as traditional chairs from High Wycombe which itself, of

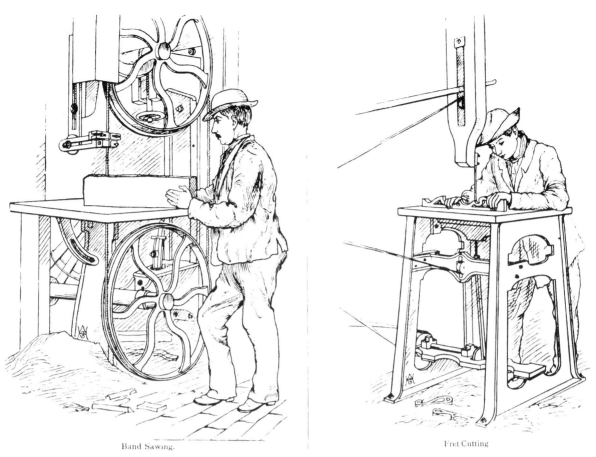

Band Sawing.   Fret Cutting

Plate 256. Mechanised band sawing and fret cutting processes in Morrison and Austin's new Steam Cabinet and Chair Works, Worship Street, London, E.C. Cabinet Maker, *March 1884.*

Incising and fluting.   Papering up.

Plate 257. Mechanised incising, fluting and 'papering up' at Morrison and Austins. Cabinet Maker, *March 1884.*

Dowel making machine, c.1895.
Courtesy Wycombe Chair Museum.

Round tenoner, c.1890.
Courtesy Wycombe Chair Museum.

course, supplied most areas. Liberty sold chairs made in Orkney whilst High Wycombe makers sent theirs to Vienna.

The receipt book of Pratts of Bradford in the 1860s shows them buying from Trapnell of Bristol, Eyles of Bath, Jenens & Bettridge of Birmingham as well as High Wycombe and London firms and there seems no reason to doubt that they continued to buy from afield in this later period when, certainly, they served as agents for Libertys.[30]

An early mail order craftsman-to-customer delivery was offered in *The Studio* in 1901 by H.T. Wyse of Arbroath who advertised his "Simple Furniture carriage paid to any railway station in Great Britain."

MECHANISATION

An account of a visit to the newly equipped Gillow factory in Lancaster in 1880 shows how far mechanisation could then go in high quality production: "We found a series of mechanical contrivances the products of which are the most perfect of their kind to be seen the world over. In addition to the usual machinery for cutting up timber from the log to the thinnest board, there are to be found machines devoted to work which is generally considered out of the power of the 'Iron-hand'. . . . in one corner is a machine for moulding and producing square legs with an exactitude that no carver could achieve. Another clever machine for planing endways of the grain is in successful operation. Machines for mortising, moulding, planing, etc. are by this time familiar to most cabinet makers; but as is well known most work affected by such means requires a good deal of handwork to finish it off. . . . These difficulties Messrs. Gillow seem to have thoroughly overcome by weight and ingenuity of mechanism, for all the work we saw issuing forth from the various machines was so clear and perfect that is scarcely required a touch of 'the paper' to finish it off. Some old fashioned cabinet makers very naturally deplore the use of machinery for their handicraft but it is evident that this express age cannot afford to wait for the labour of the hand and that those who successfully apply mechanism must lead the van in supplying the wants of the people. The workshops above the machine department afford plenty of opportunity for the display of skill on the part of the talented cabinet makers; and the various articles we saw in Jacobean, Queen Anne and Chippendale and every other fashionable style gave evidence that all kinds of work was within the grasp of these Lancashire artisans.

". . . . In these days when the decay of the apprenticeship is deplored, it is gratifying to come across an apprenticeshop in full and successful operation. A large and well lighted apartment is here devoted to the ' 'prentice hands' and a few picked men are intermixed in order to teach them their craft. . . . The modellers and carvers of the establishment have an apartment well lighted, admirably kept and profusely decorated with casts of ancient and modern decorative art. Gillows have a name for high class carving, including Renaissance work, but no foreigners are employed".[31]

LATER FACTORIES

In the 1890s more factories and machine production developed in the mechanically aware industrial towns and cities of the provinces than in London. In Scotland there was the Alexander & Co. Steam Chair Factory in Glasgow (Plate 222) and others in Glasgow and up and

168

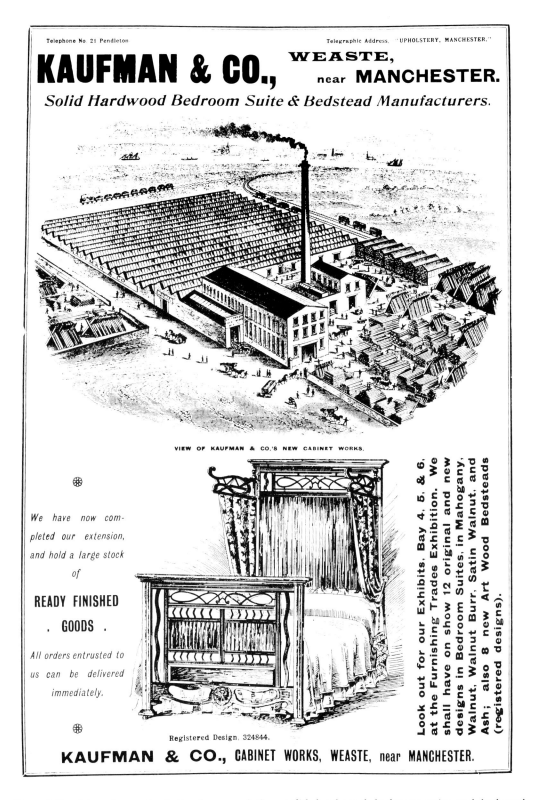

Plate 258. Advertisement of Kaufman and Co., solid hardwood bedroom suite and bedstead manufacturers, Weaste, nr. Manchester. This view of their "new cabinet works" probably includes envisaged extensions. Timber was delivered by rail from the river. The bed, registered design 324844, is described as 'New Art.' Cabinet Maker Supplement, March 15, 1899.

"AN EXPLODED IDEA"

IS WHAT THE V.P SUITE IS NOT!

BUT A PERFECT NOVELTY.

The complete Furniture of a comfortable Bedroom: 3ft. 9in. Wardrobe, 3ft. 6in. Dressing Chest, 3ft. 4in. Washstand, 2 Cane-seat Arm Chairs, Chamber Service, Bed, Bedding, &c., **FOLDS** into one small case measuring 6ft. by 2ft. 6in. by 2ft. Rigidity and appearance of glued-up Furniture. Patented all over the World. Write for Illustrated Price List to

The V.P. Folding Bedroom Suite & Furniture Co., Ltd.

Secretary : HORACE W. H. VAUGHAN.   330c, OLD ST., LONDON, E.C.

AGENTS WANTED.

Plate 259. All these items in the V.P. Suite were delivered folded into a packing case 6ft. by 2ft. 6in. by 2ft. ready for export "to all climes," 1895. Cabinet Maker, June 1896.

170

down the Clyde, notably, the Greenock Cabinet Making Co. which employed three to four hundred workers.

Kaufman and Co. (Plate 258) who specialised in bedroom furniture and James Gaymond in chairs were established in Manchester. John Lawson & Co. and Campbell Collins Liver Works were in Liverpool and the Bateman factory in Birmingham.

Some of London's largest factories seem to have been Harris Lebus which opened at Ferry Lane, Tottenham, in 1899, in addition to their Finsbury Works, Herrmanns in Limehouse, and that of C. & R. Light, the old established wholesalers of Curtain Road, who opened a bedroom suite factory with "almost unique plant of the most modern English and foreign woodworking machinery available driven by electric motors" [32] in 1898.

PROFITABILITY 1880-1915

The period opens in the middle of the trade depressions of 1873-86 and ends with the depressed years before the First War.

It is significant that in 1885 Constantine of Leeds went out of business after fifty years and the prestige firm of Jackson & Graham had to amalgamate with Collinson & Lock because "the very serious depreciation that has taken place in the rent rolls of the country and the forced economy which has been necessary among the upper ten, have not only led to a stagnation of business but have extended credit and caused bad debts to increase to a ruinous extent".[33] Perhaps it was this state of affairs which led to the closure of the very highest quality firm of Wright and Mansfield the following year.

That trade was very cut throat and competitive can be seen by comparing prices of the 70s with the distinctly lower ones in the 80s; but Kelly's 1886 *Directory* argued that the furniture trade had not suffered as much as others because of "the steady growth of the population of the kingdom . . . . the fact that the purchase of furniture must more or less be a necessity of every household, whilst the constant wear and tear and the changes incidental to fashion are constantly creating demands in the home trade" and because the export market had tripled since 1870 to not far off three quarters of a million pounds in 1886. About £400,000 of this went to the Empire with Australia and South Africa the major customers.

All grades were exported from luxury furnishings for many European hotels to "The VP suite: the complete furniture of a comfortable bedroom FOLDS into one small case 6ft by 2ft to 6in. by 2ft." (Plate 259) suitable for sending up country or to the outback on a bullock cart. More exotic orders came from further east: Jackson & Graham supplied a 14ft state bed in three divisions, the middle higher than the others, to the King of Siam in 1882.[34]

Robert Christie was allowed £40 each for impressive saloon chairs for the Czar of Russia's yacht,[35] whilst a Sheffield firm supplied a complete bedroom suite in sterling silver to an oriental customer. It consisted of a cabinet, dressing table, a dozen chairs, washing impedimenta and a bed each of whose four pillars was surmounted by a "carefully modelled" female figure 2ft 9in. in height.[36]

"Here" murmured Coffee Table, the columnist of *The Building News,* "is a suggestion for an American millionaire to improve upon."

Many firms benefited from the civic building projects of this period with hospitals, town halls, government departments and hotels to be

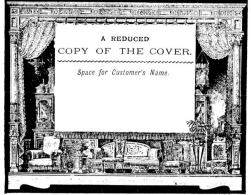
Advertisement for J. T. Norman's Furnishing Guide *("Now ready, price 10/6."), from* Cabinet Maker, *1886.*

furnished. Gillows were particularly busy with a great variety of contracts from Midland Railway Co. hotels and carriages, the Liverpool Cotton Exchange, the liners *Lusitania, Heliopolis* and *Cairo* and the Sultan's yacht to Blackpool Hospital, the Rainhill Asylum and the Adelphi Hotel, not to mention a kiosk for the Khedive in Cairo. The thousand bedroom Hotel Cecil was furnished jointly by Waring & Gillow, Shoolbreds and Maples and it was Maples who furnished Royal Holloway College in 1885.

Hire purchase facilities also must have helped trade. One of the first references to this is an advertisement by Norman & Stacey in *The Artist* in 1901 offering "A revolution in furnishing by gradual payments."

Despite the real and supposed stringencies of 'the upper ten', obviously, a good deal was spent by 'society' in Edward VII's reign when 'weekending' became such a feature of the country house scene. Many drawing rooms had to be improved and extra bedrooms and shooting boxes furnished. Lower down the scale the growing number of flats called for more compact, multi-purpose furniture.

So, trade there was, but, very competitive it had to be and, in addition, it had to meet the growing demand for novelty and variety. The designer Reg Audley bemoaned this in 1902: "The cabinet maker of today might well wish that he had lived a couple of centuries ago when people were content to be satisfied with the time honoured forms and were not constantly clamouring after novelty. In their day a job could be leisurely put through, they could take a pride in their work and prices were not 'cut' to anything like the extent to which they have to be nowadays if orders are to be obtained at all. And really if we put the whole of the designs of Chippendale, Hepplewhite and Sheraton together — designs the origination of which extended over half a century, they do not amount to more, numerically, than many cabinet makers now turn out in the course of a few months".[37]

Exports had been falling off in the 90s[38] and there was growing competition from imports, notably bentwood furniture from Austria and chairs and roll top desks from across the Atlantic. The Canadian Furniture Manufacturing Co. for example, was able to offer these at distinctly lower prices because it owned vast tracts of timber in Canada and was tooled up with the latest machinery. It is surprising to find that Belgium, which later became a considerable producer, offered no competition then and the *Building News* suggested it as a possible new outlet: "Of late years the (Belgian) manufacturers of hand-made goods have been ordering partly finished pieces (from Malines) to finish by hand and sell as 'Old Flemish'. The scarcity of wood in Belgium makes ordinary furniture expensive and it would seem that imported articles would sell well."

The article concerned with the Furniture Trade in *The Times* series: 'The Crisis in British Industry' in 1901 provides a useful first hand survey of the trade at the beginning of the twentieth century and assuming journalistic exaggeration, it may well represent the actual state of affairs some years later: "Not more than fifteen years ago London was the seat of the English furniture trade and a very large proportion of this furniture was made by garret-masters who carried on the work in their own dwellings.... The construction of new machinery by British engineers has displaced that which formerly came from the United States and Germany and has led to the practical extinction of the garret-masters and to the reorganization of the industry on its present expanded basis. Two thirds of the furniture now manufactured in Great Britain is made by machine. Not only do the machines produce sections or parts of furniture by the hundred or the thousand in a marvellously short space of time; there is the further consideration that the machines do carving and other work with the greatest accuracy. The effect of the use of machinery has been both to cheapen greatly the cost of production and greatly to increase the demand for furniture at the substantially lower prices for which it can now be obtained.

"London, too, can no longer be regarded as the seat of the industry for the great factories which have sprung up in Liverpool, Manchester, Leeds, Birmingham and elsewhere have rendered each of these towns a furniture making centre for its immediate district. As the result of this extensive resort to labour saving machines, the expansion of the industry is such that the workers are now 25% more in number than they were before the machine era set in".[39]

Perhaps it was this 25% expansion which rendered the furniture trade so vulnerable when the next trade depression came only a few years later.

In the last decade of this period there was considerable distress among small makers and many bankruptcies; and whilst many larger firms survived few can have enjoyed carefree prosperity and certainly few expanded. Even a major firm like Gillow had financial embarrassments and in May 1903 had to merge with the go-ahead Liverpool firm of Waring who also acquired the furnishing firm of Hamptons in that year. In London firms mainly declined or remained static or were absorbed into department stores as Hindleys appear to have been by Marshall & Snelgrove in 1917. Fortunately both Heals and Libertys, who had contributed so much to the progress of design, continued to thrive.

Footnotes

1. Christopher Gilbert, *Furniture History,* Vol. 12, p.42, 1976, re: Wakefield trade.
2. I am indebted to Edward Joy for this information.
3. Advertisement in Fine Art Catalogue of 1862 Exhibition, p.24.
4. J.H. Pollen, Furniture and Woodwork in *British Manu-facturing Industries,* Vol. 7, ed. G. Phillip Bevan, 1876.
5. *Furniture Gazette,* Vol. 26, p.151, May 1, 1888, survey by J.B. Lakeman.
6. J.H. Pollen, op. cit.
7. Charles Booth, *Life and Labour of the People of London,* Vol. 4; The Trades of East London connected with poverty, in the year 1888, Chapter 6. Ernest Aves: The Furniture Trade, 1893. This valuable chapter provides most of the information quoted here about conditions in the trade.
8. H.L. Williams, *The Workers Industrial Index to London,* 1881, quoted in P.G. Hall's *Industries of London since 1861,* Hutchinson's University Library, 1962. This is another useful source book.
9. *Building News,* Vol. 14, advt. p.V, January 4, 1867.
10. *Building News,* Vol. 14, p.222, March 29, 1867.
11. Fine Art Catalogue of 1862 Exhibition, p.24.
12. Gillows, *Examples of Furniture and Decoration,* c.1908, p.4.
13. *Cabinet Maker,* Vol. 1, p.52, October 1, 1880.
14. *Cabinet Maker,* Vol. 23, February 1903.
15. This and much other information gleaned from the great Booth survey, op. cit.
16. *Furniture Gazette,* Vol. 26, p.151, May 1, 1888.
17. Booth survey, op. cit., 2nd Series, Vol. 1, 1903: G.E. Arkell and G.H. Duckworth, p.182.
18. *Building News,* Vol. 16, p.120, February 5, 1869.
19. These catalogues and others were advertised in the *Cabinet Maker.*
20. In the Handley Read files in the RIBA archives.
21. *Cabinet Maker,* Vol. 1, p.88, December 1, 1880.
22. ibid.
23. Fifty one cabinet makers in Glasgow had subscribed to Thompson's *Cabinet Maker's Assistant,* 1853.
24. *Cabinet Maker,* Vol. 2, p.177, March 1, 1882.
25. *Cabinet Maker,* Vol. 5, p.80, October 1, 1884.
26. I am indebted to Edward Joy for this reference to PRO Works 21, 20/8 (1-41).
27. *Cabinet Maker,* Vol. 7, p.161, 1887.
28. Catalogue of Exhibition of Town and Country Furniture, Temple Newsam, 1972.
29. Wylie and Lochhead catalogue, c.1905-10.
30. Catalogue of Exhibition, *Victorian and Edwardian Furniture by Pratts of Bradford,* Bradford 1969-70.
31. *Cabinet Maker,* Vol. 1, November 1, 1880.
32. *Cabinet Maker,* Vol. 19, p.75, September 1898.
33. *Cabinet Maker,* Vol. 5, p.225, May 1, 1885.
34. *Building News,* Vol. 42, February 3, 1882.
35. *Cabinet Maker,* Vol. 1, p.47, 1880.
36. *Building News,* Vol. 87, p.31, July 1, 1904.
37. *Cabinet Maker,* Vol. 23, July 1902.
38. For several years in the 80s exports of 'Furnishing, Cabinet and Upholstery wares' totalled more than £700,000. By 1894 they had dropped to £418,798 but gradually rose to £636,629 by 1900. Statistics quoted in *Cabinet Maker.*
39. Quoted in *Building News,* Vol. 82, p.49, January 3, 1902.

SOME OF THE MAIN FIRMS ACTIVE DURING WHOLE OR PART OF THE PERIOD 1880-1915

Kelly's Directories of the Cabinet, Furniture and Upholstery Trades for this period are brick size volumes containing tens of thousands of names. This list gives only a few of the well established and/or more notable, with, where possible, some approximate indication of their dates and specialities. The latter are quoted mainly from London Post Office Directories.

Abbreviations: * still active in 1890   + still active in 1900   † still active in 1910

WEST END OF LONDON 1880: RETAILERS

BANTING, Thomas and Wm.
St. James Street and Wardour Street, "Upholsterers, cabinet makers, house and estate agents."

+ CHRISTIE, Robt.
George Street, Portman Square, W, cabinet maker, ". . . the high class and somewhat exclusive trade carried on by that well known house furnisher", 1883.

* COLLINSON and LOCK
Fleet Street, "manufacturers of artistic furniture and constructive woodwork for interiors", 1870. Jackson and Graham joined them in 1885. Absorbed by Gillow 1897.

*CONRATH, Fredk. John and Son
North Audley Street, "upholsterers."

COOPER, Henry and John
Great Pulteney Street, "upholsterers and art cabinet makers" from c.1875. Pioneered 'Moorish.'

COX and Sons
Southampton Street, Strand, "church (mainly) furniture manufacturers."

* CRACE, John G. and Son
Wigmore Street, "architectural decorators and manufacturers of cabinet furniture."

DOWBIGGIN, Thomas & Co.
23 Mount Street, W, "cabinet maker and upholsterer."

+ EDWARDS and ROBERTS
Wardour Street and elsewhere, "antique and modern furniture warehouse and importers of foreign cabinets."

† GILLOW and Co.
Oxford Street, "builders, painters, decorators, cabinet makers, upholsterers, carvers and gilders, bedstead and bedding manufacturers, importers of French paper hangings, silks and other fabrics, merchants, undertakers, house and estate agents." Waring and Gillow from 1903.

† GREGORY & Co.
Regent Street, "carpet manufacturer, importers of turkey, persian and indian carpets, cabinet makers, interior decorators, upholsterers and house agents."

† HAMPTON & Sons
Pall Mall East, "house furnishers and agents."

† HEAL and Son
Tottenham Court Road, "bedding, bedstead and bedroom furniture manufacturers, feather dresser and eiderdown quilt makers."

HEWETSON & MILNER
Tottenham Court Road, "house furnishers, cabinet makers, carpet and bedding manufacturers and warehousemen."

† HINDLEY, Charles & Son
Oxford Street, "carpet manufacturers, importers of turkey carpets, furniture, printers, upholsterers, cabinet makers and decorators." Became Hindley and Wilkinson 1899-1912, then Hindleys 1913-16 and, apparently, then absorbed by Marshall and Snelgrove.

† HOLLAND and Sons
Mount Street, "cabinet makers, upholsterers and decorators, house and estate agents."

* HOWARD and Sons
Berners Street, "upholsterers, decorators and cabinet makers and parquet floor manufacturers by steam power."

JACKSON and GRAHAM
Oxford Street, "upholsterers, cabinet makers, carpet manufacturers, interior decorators and importers of curtain materials and bronzes." Amalgamated with Collinson and Lock 1885.

+ JOHNSTONE and NORMAN
Bond Street, 1880-1900, cabinet makers, had a Windsor Castle contract 1889.

† LIBERTYS
Founded 1875.

MADDOX, George
21 Baker Street, "upholsterers", c.1856-1885.

† MAPLE and Co.
Tottenham Court Road, "cabinet makers, upholsterers, carpet factors and importers, decorative and general furnishers, warehousemen."

MINCHIN, Henry
Tottenham Court Road.

† MORANT, BOYD and BLANDFORD
New Bond Street, became Morant and Co, 1890, "interior decorators, painters, upholsterers, undertakers, estate and house agents, appraisers and surveyors, carvers, gilders, cabinet makers, carpet manufacturers," by appointment to Her Majesty.

† MORRIS & Co. 1862-1905 then new ownership.
Listed only as "glass painters and decorators."

ROSS, Donald
13 Denmark Street, Soho, "cabinet maker."

† SHOOLBRED, Jas.
Tottenham Court Road, "linen and woollen drapers, haberdashers, cabinet manufacturers, upholsterers, carpet warehousemen, decorators and furnishing ironmongers."

TROLLOPE, George and Sons
Halkin Street, Belgrave Square, "upholsterers."

WATT, Wm.
Grafton Street, c.1865-85, produced Godwin's designs and some by Maurice B. Adams.

† WHITELEY, Wm.
Furnisher, "the Universal Provider," The Queen's Road.

WRIGHT and MANSFIELD
104 New Bond Street, "auctioneers and estate agents, cabinet makers, interior decorators, upholsterers etc."

Plus by 1890
ALLEN and MANNOOCH
Mount Street.
BARTHOLOMEW & FLETCHER
Tottenham Court Road, upholsterers.
BENSON, W.A.S. & Co.
Office-showroom 82-3 New Bond Street (not in 1900), wholesale Dering Street depot, Eyot Works, Hammersmith.
† BOWMAN Bros.
Camden Town.
† DRUCE & Co.
Baker Street.
GRAHAM & BANKS
HEATON, J. Aldam
Designer and decorator, c.1890-1900.
† NORMAN and STACEY
House Furnishers.
† SPRIGGS, Wm. and Co.
Tottenham Court Road.
† STORY and TRIGGS
Queen Victoria Street.

Plus by 1900
ARMITAGE G. FAULKNER
18 Clifford Street, Bond Street and Stamford, Altrincham, "architectural designer and manufacturer of furniture, wrought metal, fabrics etc."
GOODYER, F.B.
New Bond Street, Regent Street, Oxford Street and Brompton Road, c.1896-1908.
GRAHAM & BIDDLE
Sole surviving partnership of Jackson and Graham.

From 1905
ELMDON & Co. Hammersmith.

EAST END: SOME OF THE LARGE WHOLESALERS
Mainly in Curtain Road, most were also makers.
† BAILEY, Wm & Son
Est. 1825, "A carefully selected stock of every description of cabinet furniture. Special attention to export orders for all climates."
† BARNET COHEN & Sons
† BOYS and SPURGE
Amboyna Works, Finsbury.
† LIGHT, Charles & Richard
Curtain Road.
+ SAUL MOSS & Sons
Est. 1840s, also upholsterers.
NORMAN, J.T.
Great Eastern Street.
SKEGG, Jas, & Son
Manufactory Rivington Street.
WALLACE, Wm. & Co.

WHOLESALE MAKERS, MAINLY EAST END
ATKINS, Edwin
Folding and fancy chair factory.
BARTHOLOMEW, Geo. & Co.
Finsbury Pavement.

BAVEYSTOCK, R.H.
Hackney, folding chair makers.
BENJAMIN, H.L.
Great Eastern Street.
DYER, HARPER & DYER (prev. DYER & WATT)
Islington, quality softwood bedroom suites.
GLIKSTEN, Jacob
HENRY, J.S.
From 1880-c.1911 Old Street, Boot Street and Hoxton, quality 'novelty' products.
HERRMANN, H.
Dod Street, Limehouse and City Road, "manufacturer of American solid black walnut and mahogany furniture, largest makers of bedroom suites in the country."
JENKS & WOOD
Holborn Viaduct.
KAHN, E. & Co.
St. Andrews Street, Holborn Circus, works Curtain Road, suppliers of 'Louis' and high quality Sheraton.
LAWES, Thos.
City Road, art furniture and overmantel manufacturer.
LAZARUS, H. & Son
Old Street, wholesale, export and retail (clubs and institutions).
LEBUS, Harris
Tabernacle Street, very large makers. Factory Tottenham.
LUCRAFT, Geo.
City Road.
MOORE & HUNTON
Finsbury Square.
NEWSON & CO.
Est. 1820s, Finsbury and Worship Street, wholesale export manufacturers and upholsterers specialising in solid and really durable furniture. Trademark a globe.
PARKER, Frederick
Bateman's Row.
SADGROVE
Est. c.1780, Finsbury.
SEWELL & SEWELL
Worship Street and London Wall.
SMEE, W. & A. & Son
Finsbury Pavement, became Smee & Cobay before 1890, very old established reliable firm.
TRIER, S. & Co.
Grays Inn Road.
WALKER, Wm.
Bunhill Row, at least since the 1860s.
WALLACE, Wm. & Co.
Wholesalers.
VOISEY, Charles
Willow Street, Finsbury. His entry stops after 1900. Did he perhaps join Smee and make the chairs stamped $\frac{CV}{S}$?

A FEW NOTABLE PROVINCIAL FIRMS
ADDINGHAM:
Wm. Brears.

ALNWICK:
T. Robertson & Sons.
AMERSHAM:
Dancer and Hearnes.
BANBURY:
Henry Stone & Sons.
BARNSTAPLE:
Shapland and Petter.
BATH:
Bath Cabinet Makers Ltd., est. 1894. Works Twerton, Bath, showrooms Berners Street, W.1.
BEITH:
John Pollock, Matthew Pollock and Robert Balfour. Matthew Pollock later joined John who had developed the West of Scotland Furniture Manufacturing Co. by 1893.
BELFAST:
Harpley and Co.
BIRMINGHAM:
F.W. Needham, manufacturer of bamboo furniture.
John Hough, Alexandra Works Woodcarving Co. Ltd, "saracenic twisted and turned lacings", 1899.
W.H. and A. Bateman's factory, a branch of Liberty (?).
BRADFORD:
C. Mills and Co.
Christopher Pratt.
BRISTOL:
Caleb Trapnell, College Green. Ellwood designed for them in 1890s.
Smith & Co, St. Augustines Parade, furnished police courts, 1884.
CHIPPING, Lancs.
H. Berry, chairmakers.
DUNDEE:
Francis East.
EDINBURGH:
Whytock and Reid.
GLASGOW:
Wylie and Lochhead.
H. and A.G. Alexander Steam Chair Factory, made the Rest-u-well spring rocker.
GREENOCK:
Greenock Cabinet Making Co. Ltd, quality products, 300-400 workers ±1900.
HALIFAX:
T. Simpson and Sons.
HIGH WYCOMBE (the list is not comprehensive):
William Birch Ltd.
W. Bartlett and Son, the Saxon chair 1898.
Benjamin North.
Nicholls and Janes.
James Cox and Son.
Thomas Glenister.
Wm. Collins.
KILMARNOCK:
Alexander and Craig, always rounded off sharp corners.

KIRKCALDY:
A.H. McIntosh.
LANCASTER:
Gillows.
LEEDS:
Marsh, Jones and Cribb, and Cavendish Sq., London.
John Reid and Sons.
Hummerston Bros.
Roodhouse and Sons.
LEICESTER:
W.T. Ellmore and Son, specialists in cane, rattan and wicker.
Jacob and Co, Atlas Works.
LIVERPOOL:
Campbell Collins, The Liver Works, West Derby.
John Lawson and Co, showroom in Hatton Gardens, London.
S.J. Waring.
LOCH WINNOCH
Joseph Johnstone.
MANCHESTER:
James Lamb 1840-1899.
Doveston, Davey, Hull & Co (to 1882 Dovestone, Bird & Hull).
E. Goodall & Co, made for Mackmurdo.
James Gaymond & Sons, chair and sofa manufacturer, "patent combined brace and double lockjointed chair."
Brentnall & Co, wholesale and export.
Kaufmann & Co.
Weaste, specialists in solid hardwood bedroom furniture.
NEWCASTLE-ON-TYNE:
Robsons Ltd, "largest and most complete house furnishers in the North of England."
NOTTINGHAM:
Wm. Lawrence.
Morris, Wilkinson and Co, "largest wicker work manufacturer in the country," 1899.
OXFORD:
Mintys, varsity chairs and sectional bookcases.
William Baker, sectional bookcases.
SALISBURY:
Arthur Foley, "one of the oldest established firms in his part of the country and has a somewhat more extended reputation as a wholesaler manufacturer principally of bedroom suites," 1880.
STOURBRIDGE:
Jos. Stringer, "well known in the Midlands," 1882.
WAKEFIELD:
Samuel Holdsworth and Sons.
WARWICK:
James Plucknett and Co, art furniture manufacturers.
WORKSOP:
Isaac Allsop and Sons.)
W. Gilling and Sons.   ) Both chairmaking firms.
YATTON:
Wake and Dean.
YORK:
Greenwoods.

Postscript 1915-40

A detailed study of the furniture of this period has yet to be written. This brief postscript, on some of the more notable and important kinds of work, is offered simply in the hope of alerting collectors to seek some of the choicer products before they too are shipped abroad.

There were few developments in furniture in Britain between 1915-25. During the 1914-18 war many firms had had to turn over to the production of ammunition boxes and some to aircraft. After the war there seems to have been an altogether understandable sense of exhaustion and lack of urge. The *Studio Year Book* of 1920 noted: "The scarcity of furniture is as notable as the shortage of houses" and because of "the vexed question of the scarcity of domestic servants ... a demand has sprung up on every hand for labour saving devices" and in favour of fitted furniture.

Gradually a few individuals moved forward. From 1922 Maurice Adams, with showrooms off Portman Square and a factory in Gloucester, was producing quality pieces with mainly unmoulded flat surfaces of highly figured walnut veneers, and in that year painted furniture by the Canal Workshops appeared. In 1923 Gordon Russell exhibited finely crafted pieces showing imaginative use of woods at prices kept down by machine assisted production.

The *Studio Year Books* until 1925 mainly illustrated craftsman-made pieces of fairly simple design. But these, as the 1925 issue pointed out, were "not appropriate for important town and suburban houses, therefore Belgravia and Hampstead will continue to prefer Chippendale and Sheraton until more appropriate alternatives are available".

But this was not the situation in parts of Europe where cubism, expressionism, vorticism and futurism were positive forces and where the influences of the Russian ballet, American Indian art and ancient Egypt were distinctly strong. In Paris the Société des Artistes-Décorateurs had been exploring these aspects since 1919 and it was in Paris, in 1925, that the immensely influential Exposition Internationale des Arts Décoratifs et Industriels Modernes was staged and what has come to be known as 'art deco' revealed. The British contribution was described as that "of isolated individuals ploughing lonely furrows in an unresponsive soil",[1] whereas, according to Sir Lawrence Weaver, the Continental exhibits suggested "a universal aesthetic emotion welcoming to novelty", with France, Austria, Holland and Sweden definitely committed to modern design.[2] The inventive French schemes were the result of close cooperation between artists, architects and craftsmen as in the D.I.M. atelier. The furniture was chiefly remarkable for the dramatic use of exotic veneers and some cubist forms.

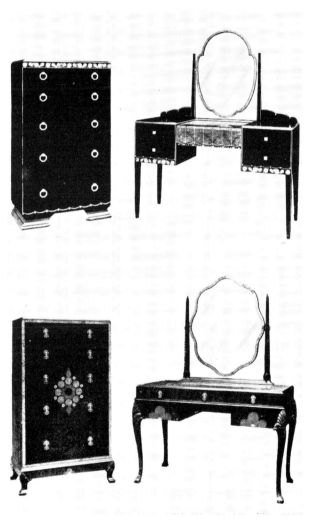

Plate 260. It was probably the above and other items in startling woods which produced a "staggering surprise for the trade" at the London Furniture Exhibition in 1926, by B. Cohen and Sons Ltd. Illustrated Studio Year Book, 1927.

Plate 261. Bedroom suite designed by C.A. Richter, made by Bath Artcraft Ltd., Bath, in amboyna, walnut, mogador and mother-of-pearl inlay. Studio Year Book, *1927.*

Its effects were seen at the London Furniture Exhibition in the following year when it was reported: "This year a new movement in furniture has been successfully launched . . . the firm that launched it, B. Cohen and Sons Ltd., produced a staggering surprise for the trade" (Plate 260) and "1926 may be regarded as a notable year so far as furniture design is concerned not so much because of the actual models produced — they represent a trial run of the movement — but because the movement really has been started". The main features of the new style were described as: "Simple lines and good proportions and an almost complete reliance for decorative effect on the woods employed: amboyna, walnut or whatever it may be. Decorative lines of inlay are also used extensively and there is ornamental punctuation by means of handles and escutcheons, in which ebony, ivory, mother-of-pearl and oxydised and gilded metal may play a part. Occasionally additional punctuation is provided by means of some small carved and gilded or silvered plaque in the centre of a panel of a sideboard, wardrobe or bed."[3]

The items in Plate 260 are probably from B. Cohen's 'Gayladye' range that caused the stir. It is difficult to think of them as startling and to share the enthusiasm but perhaps the woods themselves, the macassar ebony and the figured walnut and amboyna, were very fetching.

It was reported from the Manchester Furniture Exhibition later in 1926 that "Imagination has been released from the prison of 'period' models and although there is, of course, a large proportion of Jacobean and eighteenth century repro there is a distinct break from the conventions of design that have now ruled for many years."[4]

By September Gordon Russell and Charles Richter of Bath were exhibiting interestingly veneered pieces. Those by Richter in Plate 261 are effective designs in the new manner. As well as much decorative burr walnut some oak and mahogany were treated to intensify the grain so as to cater for "the growing taste for plain surfaces that provide their own embellishment in terms of colour and figure." Lighter finishes were given to oak and fuming was out.

In 1928 Shoolbreds mounted an exhibition of 'Modern Furniture' and it was seen that "scarcely a stand at Olympia (the Furniture Show) shows no effort on modernist lines".[5] Plate 262 shows a cabinet designed that year by Gordon Russell. Its angled arch was to be featured in the 'art deco' foyer of the Strand Palace Hotel in 1930. Plate 263 is of a traditionally moulded but dramatically veneered tallboy by J. Dugald Stark for Peter Jones Ltd. and Plate 264 an original design by Serge Chermayeff. In 1929 Chermayeff, a new designer/manager of Waring and Gillow, covered the whole of one floor of the store with a startling exhibition of modern furniture including the latest in tubular and laminated items.

Tubular steel and pliable laminated wood (as opposed to rigid laminated board) were the new exploitable materials of the late 1920s, with Marcel Breuer's first cantilevered chair in tubular steel in 1925, Alvar Aalto's first laminated chair and Mies van der Rohe's triumph, the steel bar Barcelona chair, in 1929. Techniques in metallurgy and lamination were much explored on the Continent whilst PEL (Practical Equipment Ltd.) pioneered chromium plated tubular steel in Britain. Heals, Gordon Russell Ltd. and Betty Joel Ltd. were quick to take advantage of the new possibilities and freedoms offered by bent tubes and moulded laminates.

Plate 262. Gordon Russell cabinet, on stand, the fronts of door bordered with walnut oysters enclosing burr elm quartered veneers. The interior is of ebony, yew and zebra wood, with the central niche gilt painted and drawer pulls of ivory and ebony. One of the drawers is labelled on the underside: "This piece of furniture Design No. 693 was made throughout in the Russell Workshops, Broadway, Worcs. Designer: Gordon Russell, Foreman: Edgar Turner, Cabinet Maker: I. Shilton, Metal Worker: A.L. Fry. Timber used: walnut, burr elm, yew and ebony. Date 20.7.28." 40½ inches by 57. It was made for a personal friend of Gordon Russell.
Courtesy Sotheby's Belgravia.

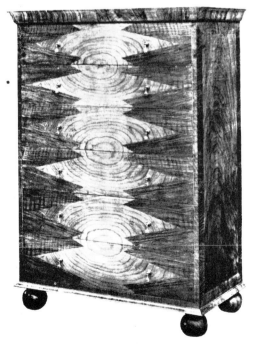

Plate 263, left: Tall boy with very striking veneers designed by J. Dugald Stark for Peter Jones. Illustrated Studio Year Book, 1928.

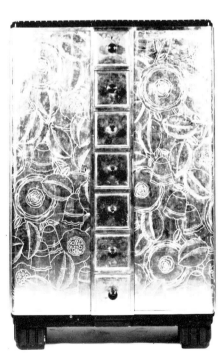

Plate 264, right. Silvered wood cabinet by Serge Chermayeff with an incised pattern of flowers, leaves and harebells on the doors, standing on dark red brown painted short frieze legs and with a painted top, 51½ins. by 34½ins. Labelled "Waring and Gillow. London, Liverpool, Manchester and Paris." 1930s.
Courtesy Sotheby's Belgravia.

Plate 265. Oval dining table veneered in French walnut with inlay of sycamore and ebony lines and plinths. Designed by Charles A. Richter. Illustrated in John Rogers, Modern English Furniture, 1930.

By 1930 there was so much work in the new manner that the furniture historian John Rogers could produce a large volume entitled *Modern English Furniture*. Plates 265-67 are from this and show sophisticated quality pieces that had been produced by then, certainly suitable for Belgravia.

Plates 268-70 are from the *Studio Year Book* of 1930. Compared with some contemporary French productions they are rather reserved examples of the new furniture, but they are in previously little used woods like macassar ebony and locust with the new accessory materials ivorine and stainless steel and new ways in veneering. The thought-provoking parquetry in Plate 268 is reminiscent of a contemporary painting by Feininger. Plate 271 shows an oak and bog oak book table made by Gordon Russell Ltd. in 1929.

Those quality pieces in Plates 265-71 were probably in limited production but Plates 272-74 show bold new items in general production by the old established High Wycombe firm of E. Gomme, c.1932. The U-shape in Plate 272, obtained by moulding a laminated sheet, was to become a characteristic form. The doors of the limed oak sideboard in Plate 273 were treated to make a powerful display of the grain and the laminations of the flattened U-shaped door frame allowed to contribute their own pattern. The 'New Cromwell' chair in Plate 274 shows the current concern with cantilevering and is exceptionally comfortable.

Plates 275-80 are from Sir Lawrence Weaver's book *High Wycombe Furniture,* published 1929. One shows some firms responding to the new ideas, another the new low 'fireside' chairs, one the preoccupation with repro and another simple modern work.

Plate 281 shows another elaborately veneered piece designed by the versatile Charles Richter, too little of whose work has yet been found. Plates 282 and 283 with their stepped forms and scalloping, but otherwise mainly unmoulded surfaces, are probably of the mid-30s.

Unfortunately the ziggurat and other stepped forms, the zigzags, electric flash motifs, sunbursts and other features in the art deco

Plate 266. Sideboard in figured mahogany with ebony bandings and plinths. Designed by Charles A. Richter. Illustrated in John Rogers, Modern English Furniture, 1930.

vocabulary were all too frequently and irrelevantly splattered on to a vast amount of poor quality, flashily veneered furniture so that the reputation of the 30s has been badly smeared. With the over-production of this over-glossy 'jazz modernistic' and a lot of shoddy repro mish-mash known in the trade as 'Jaco-bethan', it is not surprising few remember that some very finely crafted exciting modern work was also produced then. It is for this that the search is now on.

The final Plate, 284, showing a cabinet designed c.1930 by J.H. Sellers, serves as a reminder that in the background individual designers and designer craftsmen were producing pieces remarkable for their fine craftsmanship, displaying the merits and possibilities of carefully chosen woods, rather than for any advances in design.

The following is a list of some of those craftsmen and designers who continued to create high quality furniture made mainly by hand:

> Ernest Gimson (d.1919) of Sapperton
> Peter Waals who carried on his workshop
> Sidney Barnesley, and his son Edward,
>   of Sapperton and later Petersfield
> J.H. Sellers
> Joseph Armitage
> Percy Wells
> Charles Spooner
> Arthur Simpson of Kendal
> A. Rowney Green
> Stanley Davies, his pupil of Windermere
> Edward Gardiner, near Rugby
> Ernest Joyce of Brenchley
> Theo Dalrymple of Newmarket and Huntingdon
> Robert Thompson of Kilburn
> R.V.K. Townsend of Saxmundham

Footnotes

1. *Studio Year Book,* 1926.
2. *Studio Year Book,*1927.
3. *Cabinet Maker,* 1926, quoted in Jubilee issue May 4, 1935.
4. ibid.
5. ibid.

Plate 267. Writing table in walnut and ebony. The plinths project while the frieze and top are inset. Designed by R.W. Symonds and Robert Lutyens and illustrated in John Rogers, Modern English Furniture, *1930.*

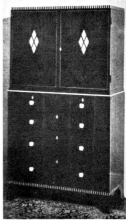

Plate 268. Chest, left, in mahogany veneered with French walnut, base of walnut and canted ends veneered with darker figured walnut. Designed and produced by B. Cohen and Sons Ltd., London. Veneering of lower section suggests a Feininger painting. The dark chest in macassar ebony and ivory on laminated gaboon designed by Shirley B. Wainright, the co-editor of Studio Yearbook where both these chests were illustrated, 1930.

Plate 270. Sideboard in English walnut with handles and unusual pedestal supports in stainless steel, designed by J. Emberton, ARIBA, and made by Bath Cabinet Makers' Co. Ltd., Bath. Illustrated Studio Year Book, *1930.*

Plate 269. Dramatic dressing table in locust wood, with inlaid bands of ivorine. Designed by C.A. Richter and made by The Bath Cabinet Makers' Co., Bath. Illustrated Studio Year Book.

Plate 271, left. Square oak book table with cut away corners. The base is of bog oak. About ten were made. Gordon Russell Ltd., 1929.

Plate 272, right. Draw table of heavy construction and made in oak, limed or antique. The insignificant low relief carved decoration sometimes picked out in colour. 4ft. by 3ft. closed, 6ft. by 3ft. open. Rounded corners. £9 15s. Made by E. Gomme, High Wycombe, c.1932.

Plate 273, left. Oak sideboard limed or antique, 54ins. wide, 58ins. overall, contains four drawers and storage for bottles and glass right, shelf on left. £15 10s. 6d. Made by E. Gomme, High Wycombe.

Plate 274. The 'New Cromwell' armchair, "not a freak" announced the catalogue. Limed or antique with leather cloth seat. The arms, together with the one piece bent-wood seat rail, are housed in solid ends. The same petty carving on ends near arms, stained green, £1 18s. 6d. Design registered by E. Gomme. No. 778034.

Plate 275. Turning and rush make an interesting modern chair of broad proportions in (a); the Gothic flavour of (b) is marked and (c) is built of a pleasant mixture of weathered oak and ash. Of the bottom row, (k) has perhaps the most distinguished ancestry, for it is an exact replica of a late eighteenth century Library Chair; (g) and (h) are simple and popular upholstered straight-backed arm-chairs.

Plate 276. Of all modern chairs the little low fireside chair is the most recent and has given infinite opportunity for various treatment. The Windsor has given the idea for (a), but it is not wholly "Windsor" in construction. Example (b) is a cross between the ancient X chair and the bow-back Windsor, with drum-stretched hide, filling the entire bow; (d) has a rather austere Cromwellian look and (e) has a hint of Chippendale in miniature.

Plates 275-280 with text are taken from High Wycombe Furniture, by Sir Lawrence Weaver, 1929.

Plate 277. Chairs (a) and (b) are interesting small oak dining chairs with hide seats. In (a) the slats run up straight and then change to a curve, conforming with the curve of the top rail; in (b) hide straps are interlaced with a single slat. Example (c) is of a more traditional form with hair seat. The sideboard (d) is an admirably simple piece of interesting form and restrained detail.

Plate 278. Sideboard (a) is a modern adaptation of Gothic form and decoration and is in oak with rather dim colour in the carved ornament. Example (b) is an interesting exercise in the Jacobean manner with decoration so devised that it can be worked wholly on the machine with fretsaw and spindle. Despite the absence of handwork and the essential novelty of the decoration the piece worthily presents a traditional character.

Plate 280. Wooden bedsteads give the designer great opportunity of invention and High Wycombe has not been slow to show its versatility in this regard. Example (a) is inlaid with a strong angular treatment of spaces; (b) is inventive rather in form, because the foot of the bed forms a useful double-door cupboard; (c) is wholly modern, covered with leather decorated somewhat in the Cordova manner and (d) is covered entirely with chintz.

Plate 279. The purely modern treatment of the bookcase (a) and writing-table (b) owes its success to austere lines and the fine workmanship of the structure, the rich walnut veneer and delicate King Wood banding and inlay.

Plate 281. Bath Cabinet Makers' Co. walnut sideboard with diamond parquetry veneers. One cupboard contains a lead lined cellarette. 66ins. wide. The table en suite is labelled 'Bath Cabinet Makers' Co. Ltd.,' with a transfer of the arms of the City of Bath inscribed 'Authorized by the City', 1930s. C.A. Richter was then a designer and executive of the Company.
Courtesy Sotheby's Belgravia.

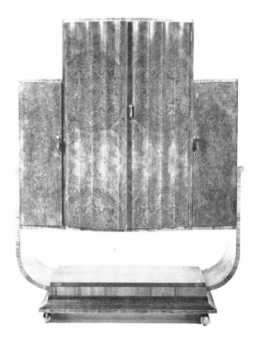

Plate 283. Walnut cocktail cabinet. The raised central section has rippled doors enclosing a satin-birch mirrored interior with cupboard and drinks slide. It is held up by moulded laminated out curving supports rising from a rectangular lower tier on castors. 67ins. by 49ins., c.1930.
Courtesy Sotheby's Belgravia.

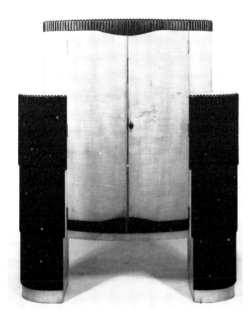

Plate 282. Stylish cocktail cabinet veneered in birchwood, of oval section with projecting block hemispherical legs cased in stepped and reeded ebonized wood. The doors open on to twin shelves above a compartment fitted for glasses and bottles, a sliding smoked glass work surface, further fittings and electric light. Labelled 'Caplans, Furnishing Craftsmen of Excellence.'
Courtesy Sotheby's Belgravia.

Plate 284. Mahogany cabinet on stand designed by J. Henry Sellers, c.1930. The shaped apron of the lower tier is characteristic of his attention to detail.
Courtesy Sotheby's Belgravia.

A Partial Bibliography

RELEVANT TO 1880-1915

PATTERN BOOKS AND DRAWINGS

1867   Bruce J. Talbert, *Gothic Forms Applied to Furniture.*

1875   B.E. Smith, *Designs and Sketches for Furniture in the New Jacobean style.*

1876   Bruce J. Talbert, *Examples of Ancient and Modern Furniture.*

1877-89   *Cabinet Makers' Pattern Book,* 1st series 1877. *Cabinet Makers' Pattern Book,* 3rd series 1882. *Cabinet Makers' Pattern Book,* 5th series n.d.

1877-79   A. Jonquet, *Original Sketches for Art Furniture.*

1878   The Practical Cabinet Maker, *A collection of working drawings with notes by a Working Man.*

1878   R. Charles (of Wigan), *The Compiler.*

1878   W.G. and G.A. Audsley, *Outlines of Ornament in all styles.*

1880   A. Sedley, *A few hints on Cabinet Work.*

1880   *Fashionable Furniture, a collection of 350 original sketches,* by the late Bruce Talbert and H. Shaw, A. Jonquet, W. Scott Morton, W. Timms, J. Ward, C. Porter, A.E. Robinson, W. Hamer, J. Breckin, E. Foley, published by *Cabinet Maker.*

1882   *Furniture Trades Catalogue,* 3rd series.

1882   J. Moyr-Smith, *Album of Decorative Figures.*

1882   Frederick Schwenke, *Designs for Decorating Furniture and Modern Chamber Arrangements* (mainly Continental).

1883   H.W. Batley, *A series of Studies for Domestic Furniture.*

1883   John W. Small, *Ancient and Modern Furniture,* pub. Edinburgh.

1885   Owen W. Davis, *Art and Work* (he designed for Gillow and Shoolbred).

1885   R.S. Pullan (ed.), *The Designs of William Burges.*

1888   Maurice B. Adams, FRIBA, *Examples of Old English Houses and Furniture with some modern works from designs by the author.*

1889   Robert Brook, *Elements of Style in Furniture and Woodwork.*

1890   A. Jonquet, *Present Day Furniture.*

c.1900   *Bedroom furniture designs with scale drawing,* pub. Evans Bros.

1904   William Timms and Webb, *Thirty Five Styles of Furniture.*

1904   Herbert Binstead, *The Furniture Styles.*

1904   R. Davis Benn, *Style in Furniture.*

1906   H.E. Binstead, *Useful Details in Several Styles.*

1909   *Style Schemes in Antique Furnishing Interiors and their treatment* written by H.P. Shapland, the schemes designed by H. Pringuer Benn. Gillow Estimate and Sketch Books for almost all this period in Westminster Public Library. Collection of Furniture drawings by C.F.A. Voysey in RIBA Library.

Stuart Durant, *Victorian Ornamental Design,* pub. Academy editions 1972, a collection.

TRADE CATALOGUES

1862   George Maddox, *Illustrated catalogue of Bedroom Furniture and the new Exhibition Chamber Furniture.*

1871   Collinson and Lock, *Sketches for Artistic Furniture.*

c.1872   William Collins, Downley, High Wycombe, "manufacturer of all kinds of Cane and Fancy Chairs in Birch, Cherry, Sycamore, Walnut, Oak and Mahogany woods or in imitation of the above woods," *Catalogue.*

c.1872   Oetzmann & Co., *A guide to house furnishing.*

1874   J. Shoolbred and Co., *Designs for furniture.*

1879   Blyth and Sons, *Designs of cabinet furniture.*

1881   C. and R. Light, *Cabinet Furniture.*

1882   *Furniture Trades Catalogue,* 3rd series.

1882   George Maddox, *Catalogue of Furniture.*

1883   Heal, *Catalogue of Bedsteads and Furniture.*

1883   Hewetson and Milner, *Illustrated catalogue.*

1885   Oetzmann and Co., *Trade Catalogue.*

1885   Whiteley's *Catalogue.*

1889   J. Shoolbred, *Illustrated Catalogue.*

1892   Hampton and Sons, *Catalogue of Stock.*

c.1893-1910   Liberty, *Yuletide catalogues,* and others n.d.

1894   J.S. Henry. 6- or 8-page booklet with coloured illustrations.

1895	Harrod's *Catalogue*.	
1896	Heal, *Bedsteads, Bedding and Bedroom Furniture*.	
1897	Oetzmann and Co., *Guide to House Furnishing*, 750pp.	
1890s	J. Aldam Heaton, *Design and Decoration including Chimney Pieces, Glass and Decoration and Furniture*.	
late 1890s	Maples, *Useful Articles suitable for presents*.	
1898	H.L.L. (Harris Lebus, London).	
1900	*A Bedroom furnished by Heal and Son for the Paris Exhibition*.	
c.1900	S. and S. (Sewell and Sewell), *Catalogue*, 1080pp.	
c.1900	Robson and Son, Newcastle-on-Tyne, *Chimney Pieces*.	
c.1900	B.C. and S. (Barnet, Cohen and Son), *Selected designs for Artistic Furniture*.	
c.1900	Hampton and Son, *Designs for Furniture and Decoration and Complete House Furnishings*.	
1900	Henry Turner Wyse, *Simple Furniture*, pub. Arbroath, 2nd ed. 1901.	
c.1900	Story and Trigg, *Special Furnishings*.	
1901	S.J. Waring and Sons, *The new note in furnishing*.	
1901	Gillow, *Record of a Furnishing Firm during two centuries*.	
1901	J.P. White, *Furniture made at the Pyghtle Works, Bedford*, designed by M.H. Baillie Scott.	
1901	Jacques Housez, *Art Furniture Design Book*, 100 copies privately printed in Bristol.	
1904	Heal, *Reproductions of early Georgian Bedroom Furniture*.	
1904	Maples, *Book of Chairs*.	
1904	Hampton's *Antiques*.	
1905	Elmdon and Co., *Illustrated catalogue of designs by Charles Spooner and Arthur J. Penty* (the proprietors).	
1906	Liberty, *Simple and Durable Furniture at Modest Cost*.	
1906	Maples, *Illustrations of Furniture*, 944 pp.	
1906	Norman and Stacey, *Notes on artistic house furnishing*.	
1900+	Wylie and Lochhead, important catalogue, very comprehensive.	
	Whiteley's, *Illustrated Furnishing Catalogue* (between 1893-1904).	
	Liberty, *Handbook of Sketches for Dining Room and Library Furniture*, n.d.	
c.1906-12	Hindley and Wilkinson, *Catalogue*.	
1907	*Catalogue of a Private Collection of Antique and Modern Furniture* issued by Hindley and Wilkinson.	

1907	Liberty, *Inexpensive furniture*.
1908	Waring and Gillow, *Examples of Furniture and Decoration*.
1909	Liberty, *Upholstered Chairs*.
1909	Morris and Co., *Catalogue of designs of George Jack*.
c.1910	Wolfe and Hollander, *House Decoration and Furniture*.
1910	Norman and Stacey, *Catalogue of Artistic Furniture*.
1910	J.S. Henry, *Catalogue of repro pieces*.
1910-11	Liberty, *Reproductions of 17th century furniture*.
1911	Liberty, *Reproductions of Old English Furniture*.
1912	Morris and Co., *Specimens of Upholstered Furniture*.
	(N.B. when 'Decorators' added after Morris and Co., catalogue is post-1905 when the business was sold.)
1912	Morris and Co., *Illustrated notices*.
1915	Omega Work Shops Ltd., pamphlet.
1930	E. Pollard and Co., *Catalogue of exhibition of furniture designed by Frank Brahgwyn (contains some pre-1915 designs)*.

CONTEMPORARY BOOKS ON TASTE AND STYLE

1868	C.L. Eastlake, *Hints on Household Taste*.
1875	Anon., *Tables and Chairs*, a practical guide to Economical Furnishing in 'The Useful Library'.
1876	H.J.C. (Cooper), *The Art of Furnishing*.
1876-78	Art in the Home Series: W.J. Loftie, *A Plea for Art in the House*; Mrs. Lucy Orrinsmith, *The Drawing Room*, 1877; Rhoda and Agnes Garrett, *Suggestions for House Decoration*, 1877; Mrs. Loftie, *The Dining Room*, 1878; Lady Barker, *The Bedroom and The Boudoir*, 1878.
1875-76	Christopher Dresser, *Studies in Design*.
1878	William Morris, *The Decorative Arts, their relation to Modern Life and Progress*.
1879	Anon., *A House and its furniture, a commonsense guide to House Building and House Furnishing, with illustrations*.
1880	Anon., *Artistic Homes*.
1881	R.W. Edis, *Decoration and Furniture of Town Houses*.
1882	Christopher Dresser, *Art of Decorative Design*.
1882	Lucy Crane, *Art and the formation of Taste*.
1884	Mrs. Gladstone, *Healthy Nurseries and Bedrooms*.
1886	Christopher Dresser, *Modern Ornamentation*.
1886	Edward Morse, *Japanese Homes and their surroundings*.

1887   J. Moyr Smith, *Interior Decoration.*

1889   Mrs. H.R. Haweis, *The Art of Decoration,* new edition.

1893   E. Knight, *Taste and Economy in Decoration and Ornament.*

1893   *Arts and Crafts Essays* – by members of the Arts and Crafts Exhibition Society.

1893   C. Pratt, *Hints on House Furnishing.*

1897   Edith Wharton and Ogden Codman, *The Decoration of Houses.*

1897   Rosamund Marriott Watson, *The Art of the House.*

1897   Aldham Heaton, *Beauty and Art.*

1898   Gleeson White, *A note on simplicity of design in furniture.*

1901   C. Holme (ed.), *Modern British Architecture and Decoration,* special number of *The Studio.*

1902   H.J. Jennings for Waring and Gillow, *Our Homes and how to beautify them.*

1904   W. Shaw Sparrow, *The British Home of Today.*

1905   W. Shaw Sparrow, *The Modern Home.*

1906   M.H. Baillie Scott, *Houses and Gardens.*

1907   J.H. Elder-Duncan, *The House Beautiful and Useful.*

1909   W. Shaw Sparrow, *Hints on House Furnishing.*

1909   C.R. Ashbee, *Craftsmanship in Competitive Industry.*

1911   Mable Tuke Priestman, *Artistic Homes.*

1913   W. Godfrey, *The Art and Craft of Home-making.*

CONTEMPORARY CRITICAL AND FACTUAL WORKS

1878   W.J. Audsley, *Popular Dictionary of Architecture and Allied Arts,* Liverpool.

1878   G.W. Yapp, *Art, Industry, Furniture and Metalwork,* 2 vols.

1882   W. Hamilton, *The Aesthetic Movement.*

1890   C.R. Ashbee, *Transactions of the Guild and School of Handicraft.*

1892   F. Litchfield, *Illustrated History of Furniture,* chapter 9.

1902   Ernst Wasmuth, *Turin 1902, views of the Exhibition.*

1905   H. Muthesius, *Der Innerraum des Englischen Hauses.*

WORKS ON THE FURNITURE TRADE

Kelly's Directory of Cabinet, Furniture and Upholstery Trades, 2nd edition 1886, 3rd 1894, 4th 1899, 5th 1903, 6th 1907.

G. Philip Bevan (ed.), *British Manufacturing Industries,* chapter by J.H. Pollen: Furniture and Woodworking, 1876.

H.L. Williams, The *Workers' Industrial Index to London,* 1881.

Charles Booth, *Life and Labour of the People of London, Vol. 4; The Trades of E. London connected with poverty in the year 1888,* Chapter 6. Ernest Aves: The Furniture Trade.

H.B. Wheatley and P. Cunningham, *London Past and Present,* 1891, 3 vols.

Cheapwood Co., *Price List of woods and goods,* c.1891.

J.H. Bardwell and others, *Two Centuries of Soho,* by the clergy of St. Annes, 1898.

Arthur Morrison, *Child of the Jago* (a novel set among East End workshops c.1900).

Williamson and Son, *A survey of old furnishings in a country town,* Guildford, c.1908.

R.H. Hall, *Industries of London since 1861,* 1962.

John L. Oliver, *The Development and Structure of the furniture industry,* 1966.

L. John Mayes, *History of Chairmaking in High Wycombe,* 1966.

PERIODICALS

1842-   *The Builder,* a weekly "for Architect, Engineer, Archaeologist, Constructor, Sanitary Reformer and Art lover." (A George Godwin its editor in 1880s, his views sound like E.W. Godwin's – his brother?)

1856-   *Building News.*

1849-1912   *Art Journal.*
      Fifty Years of Art 1849-99, being articles and illustrations from the Art Journal, 1900, ed. D. Croal Thomson.

1873-94   *Furniture Gazette.*

1873-83   *Art Workman.*

1878-   *Magazine of Art.*

1880-   *Cabinet Maker and Art Furnisher,* a monthly; became *Cabinet Maker and Complete House Furnisher* and after 1905 a weekly less concerned with design.

1880-94   *The Artist and Journal of Home Culture.*

1880-1902   *The Artist,* an illustrated monthly record of the Arts, Crafts and Industries.

1880-93   *Decoration in Painting, Architecture, Furniture.*

1881   *Journal of Decorative Art.*

1884   *The Hobby Horse,* the journal of the Century Guild.

1890-99   *Furnisher and Decorator.*

1893-   *The Studio.*

1896-   *Architectural Review.*

1897   *The House.*

1899   *The Furnisher.*

1902-6   *Art Workers' Quarterly.*

1904   *Arts and Crafts.*

BOOKS OF INSTRUCTIONS

1872	J. Richards, *A Treatise on the Construction and Operation of Woodworking Machines.*
1890s	D. Denning, *Cabinet Making,* n.d.
1893	W.A.S. Benson, *Elements of Handicraft and Design, a young people's handbook.*
1898	J.P. Arkwright, *Cabinet Making for Amateurs.*
1899	Stephen Webb, *Intarsia* in *Journal of Society of Arts,* Vol. 5.
1903	George Jack, *Woodcarving, design and workmanship.*
1908	*Modern Carpenter, Joiner and Cabinet Maker,* 8 vols.
1909	Paul N. Hasluck, *Cabinet Work and Joinery.*
1909	P.A. Wells and John Hooper, *Modern Cabinet Work, Furniture and Fitments.*
	E.J. Wiseman, *Victorian Do-It-Yourself,* extracts from *Amateur Work Illustrated 1881-91* "for the clerk, the curate, the struggling professional man and the man of letters."

AUTOBIOGRAPHIES, REMINISCENCES, BIOGRAPHIES AND BACKGROUND

1882	Benjamin North, *Autobiography.*
	James Hopkinson, *A Victorian Cabinet Maker 1819-94.*
1896	F. Maddox Hueffer, *F. Maddox Brown, a Record of his Life and Work.*
1897	Aylmer Vallance, *William Morris.*
1907	Walter Crane, *An Artist's Reminiscences.*
1910	W.S. Sparrow, *Frank Brangwyn and his work.*
1911	Walter Crane, *William Morris to Whistler.*
1924	W. Lethaby and Others, *Ernest Gimson, his life and work,* Shakespeare Head Press.
1932	R. Blomfield, *W.R. Lethaby.*
1935	W.R Lethaby, *Phillip Webb.*
1935	H.J.L. Massé, *The Art Workers' Guild.*
1949	Dudley Harbron, *The conscious stone, a biography of E.W. Godwin.*
1957	John Branden-Jones, *Voysey, a memoir* in *Architectural Assoc. Journal,* May 1957.
	Greaves and Thomas, *The Golden Jubilee of Greaves and Thomas 1905-55.*
	Holbrook Jackson, *The Eighteen Nineties.*
	Richard J. Lamb, *William Whiteley, the Universal Provider.*
	John Betjeman, *Summoned by Bells* (for firm of G. Betjeman, Clerkenwell).
1965	Bea Howe, *Arbiter of Elegance* (Mrs. Haweis).
1973	Norman Jewson, *By chance I did rove* (reminiscences about Gimson).
1975	Alison Aldburgham, *Liberty's, a biography of a shop.*
1976	Andrew Saint, *Norman Shaw.*

BOOKS OF USE TO REPRODUCERS

Many in the Pattern Book section and antiquarian works such as:

1836	H. Shaw, *Specimens of Ancient Furniture.*
1844	George Fildes, *Elizabethan Furniture.*
1865	Owen Jones, *Grammar of Ornament.*
1875	John H. Pollen, *Ancient and Modern Furniture and Woodwork in the South Ken. Museum.*
1878	John Small, *Scottish woodwork of the Sixteenth and Seventeenth Centuries* (measured drawings).
1881	A Batsford reprint of *Architecture, Decoration and Furniture of R. and J. Adam.*
1883	John Small, *Ancient and Modern Furniture.*
1883	William Bliss Saunders, *Examples of Carved Oak.*
1888	Arthur Marshall, *Specimens of Carved Furniture and Woodwork.*
1888	William Sharp Ogden, *Examples of Antique Furniture, mainly 17th century.*
1888	G.J. Oakeshott, *Detail and Ornament of the Renaissance.*
1895	Complete reprint of 3rd edit. Sheraton's *Drawing Book,* Gibbings and Co.
1898	Alfred E. Chancellor, *Examples of Old Furniture English and Foreign.*
1903	J. Weymouth Hurrell, *Measured drawings of old oak English Furniture.*
1903	Fred Roe, *Ancient Coffers and Cupboards.*
1903	F. Hamilton Jacks, *Handbook for designers and craftsmen: Intarsia and Marquetry.*

BIBLIOGRAPHICAL WORKS

1885	*List of books in the National Art Library illustrating furniture* (South Kensington Museum), 2nd edition, 66 pp.
1908	*Bulletin of the New York Public Library* (September) including List of Works in the N.Y. Library relating to Furniture and Decoration.
1927	*Grand Rapids List of Books on Furniture.*
1929	*List of books in the Detroit Public Library Fine Art Dept. on Furniture.*
1952	Victoria and Albert Museum *Catalogue of Exhibition of Victorian and Edwardian Decorative Arts* by Peter Flood (contains valuable book lists).
1965	Ben Weinreb Ltd. catalogue, *Furniture.*
1972	Jeremy Cooper, *Victorian Furniture,* an introduction to the sources and a bibliography, *Apollo,* Vol. XCV, February 1972.
1975	Ben Weinreb Ltd., catalogue 29, *The Arts Applied* by Denise Chafer and Hugh Pagan.

RECENT WORKS

1952   Thomas Haworth, *Charles Rennie Mackintosh and the Modern Movement.*

1953   David Joel, *The Adventure of British Furniture 1851-1951.*

1958   *Early Victorian, Connoisseur Period Guides,* Peter Floud: Furniture.

1960   Nicholas Pevsner, *Pioneers of Modern Design,* rev. ed.

1962   Elizabeth Aslin, *19th Century Furniture.*

1962   R.W. Symonds and B.B. Whineray, *Victorian Furniture.*

1965   Charles Handley Read, *England 1830-1901* in *World Furniture,* ed. Helena Hayward.

1966   Mario Amaya, *Art Nouveau.*

1968   Charles Handley Read, *High Victorian Design,* 6th Conference Report of Victorian Society.

1966   Ella Moody, *Modern Furniture.*

1968   Simon Jervis, *Victorian Furniture.*

1968   Robert Macleod, *Charles Rennie Mackintosh.*

1968   *Charles Rennie Mackintosh Furniture,* a catalogue of the Glasgow School of Art Collection.

1968   Nicholas Pevsner, *Studies in Art, Architecture and Design,* Vol. 2.

1969   Elizabeth Aslin, *The Aesthetic Movement: Prelude to Art Nouveau.*

1971   Gillian Naylor, *Arts and Crafts Movement.*

1972   *Victorian and Edwardian Decorative Arts,* The Handley Read Collection Exhibition catalogue.

1972   Edward Joy, *Furniture,* Connoisseur Illustrated Guides, Chapters 7 and 8.

1972   James D. Kornwolf, *M.H. Baillie Scott and the Arts and Crafts Movement,* John Hopkins Press, Baltimore.

1974   Filippo Alison, *Charles Rennie Mackintosh as a designer of chairs.*

1974   James Mackay, *Dictionary of turn of the century antiques.*

1974   Phillipe Garner, *The World of Edwardiana.*

1975   Alastair Service, *Edwardian Architecture and its Origins.*

1976   Robin Spencer, *The Aesthetic Movement.*

1976   Nicholas Cooper, *The Opulent Eye.*

1977   Mark Girouard, *Sweetness and Light: The Queen Anne Movement 1860-1900.*

1978   Gillian Walking, *Bamboo Furniture.*

Index